I0811482

Praise for

Speaking Their Language

"*Speaking Their Language* is such a timely resource for the disciple-making church. If you and your church are interested in learning how you can connect to the particular cultures around your ministry setting with the gospel, then this is the best book you can read this year. It's been a long time since the PCUSA had such a clear voice to help the church in need of revitalization and renewal. Jason Tucker is the new strong voice in revitalization, and you will be glad you allowed him to coach you and your church."

—**Dr. Tom Cheyney**, Founder and Directional Leader, The Renovate Group

"Not a typical change-your-church book. I love how Jason's faith, vulnerability, and personal experiences make church relevancy actually doable! With a refreshing combination of insights, empowerment, and inspiration, this accessible, can-do guide offers practical help and hope. Like a fun mentor, Jason's warm and winsome conversational style promises to equip your church to come alive and make a relevant difference. Jason's book is definitely *not* a dry read. It'll quench your thirst for practical insights that can change your church if you let it!"

—**Joani Schultz**, Former Chief Creative Officer, Group Publishing; coauthor of *Why Nobody Wants to Go to Church Anymore*

"This book offers real-world insights from someone who didn't just study church revitalization; he lived it. After completing doctoral studies in the field, Dr. Tucker revitalized his church and then successfully coached others. You will find easy-to-grasp and proven principles that can help give new life to almost any church."

—**Bob Whitesel**, DMin, PhD, foresight strategist, church leadership professor/author, equipping churches for what's next at www.Leadership.Church

"Finally—a practical, hope-filled guide for every church longing to engage the next generation without losing the heart of their congregation. If your heart beats to reach younger generations, *Speaking Their Language* is a must-read. With clarity, encouragement, and down-to-earth practicality, it offers a clear path for inviting young people into a lifelong adventure with Jesus and his Church. Most churches cling to what's familiar—repeating last year's programs because they feel safe, even as they struggle to engage younger generations without alienating older ones. With warmth, insight, and actionable wisdom, Jason Tucker offers a hopeful and realistic way forward."

—**E. Stanley Ott**, PhD, President of the Vital Churches Institute, coauthor of the podcast *Building One Another*

SPEAKING *their* LANGUAGE

Leading Your Church to Reach Younger Generations

JASON TUCKER

LEAFWOOD PUBLISHERS
an imprint of Abilene Christian University Press

SPEAKING THEIR LANGUAGE
Leading Your Church to Reach Younger Generations

LEAFWOOD PUBLISHERS
an imprint of Abilene Christian University Press

ISBN 978-1-68426-263-2 | LCCN 2025021177

Printed in the United States of America

Published in association with The Blythe Daniel Agency, Inc., PO Box 64197, Colorado Springs, CO 80962.

LIBRARY OF CONGRESS CATALOGING-IN-PUBLICATION DATA
Names: Tucker, Jason, 1973- author
Title: Speaking their language : leading your church to reach younger generations / Jason Tucker.
Description: Abilene, Texas : Leafwood Publishers, [2026] | Includes bibliographical references.
Identifiers: LCCN 2025021177 (print) | LCCN 2025021178 (ebook) | ISBN 9781684262632 paperback | ISBN 9781684268160 ebook
Subjects: LCSH: Church work with youth | Christian leadership
Classification: LCC BV4447 .T82 2026 (print) | LCC BV4447 (ebook)
LC record available at https://lccn.loc.gov/2025021177
LC ebook record available at https://lccn.loc.gov/2025021178

Cover design by Greg Jackson, Thinkpen Design
Interior text design by Michael Flatt

Leafwood Publishers is an imprint of Abilene Christian University Press.
ACU Box 29138
Abilene, Texas 79699

1-877-816-4455
www.leafwoodpublishers.com

26 27 28 29 30 31 // 6 5 4 3 2 1

To my amazing wife, Karin; our incredible kids, Katie, Jason, and Jacob; my sister, Susie; my brother, Nick; and my mom, Katie (1949–99).

Contents

Preface

It's a little weird that my call to professional ministry happened three days before I knew Jesus. It's also a little weird that I wrote a novel as my senior project at Allegheny College in 1995 and am just now getting a book published. (To be fair, the novel was terrible.) That said, God's timing is a funny thing.

This book has been a labor of love thirty years in the making. It comes from a desire to see the church flourish again. It's where God is made known, where lives are transformed, and where people discover their identity and purpose. The church is the hope of the world. It's where kingdom-of-heaven promises meet kingdom-of-the-world problems. But the church is also a dang mess (in case you didn't notice). It makes me crazy sometimes, mostly because it doesn't have to be this way.

Over the last thirty years, whether as a worship leader, youth pastor, speaker, church coach, or senior pastor, I've seen the church fighting the same battles over and over again. Most of those battles are with itself. A church is either struggling to adjust to the changing culture around it or pretending that no adjustment is necessary. It's only a matter of time before churches that choose the latter close their doors. Even those that do adjust need to adjust the right things, or they'll be soon to follow.

My heart compels me to help churches figure this out. This book lays out a process that will help any church of any size do exactly that. This 4D Process, which I developed over the last six years, is the same process I used to help revitalize my own church, as well as dozens of other churches across the country. It's based upon the work of church consultant Bob Whitesel. I'm incredibly grateful for his guidance and friendship along the way (it's only fitting that he was the first guest on *The Reclaimed Leader* podcast).

While this book will deliver the process, you might find a workbook to be helpful. So, I created one for you to use as a supplement; it can be found at www.reclaimedleader.com/translation. I pray that it helps you lead, grow, and increase the impact of your church in your community.

Acknowledgments

I would first like to thank Leafwood Publishers for giving me the opportunity to get this resource out to pastors, leaders, and devoted members who hunger for a more faithful and fruitful church (and for knowledge of how to do it).

I also want to thank my friend and colleague Jesse Skiffington, cohost of *The Reclaimed Leader* podcast. When we hit the record button in 2017, I never imagined the impact it would have on my own life and leadership. If not for those weekly conversations, I don't know if I would've even made it this far. I certainly would not be the leader I am today.

I'd like to thank my ministry colleagues, including Bob Whitesel for his friendship, guidance, and teaching, and all the pastors whom I've shared the journey with over the years, especially Pastor Theresa, who has worked with me for over a decade.

I'd like to thank my church family at Tower Hill Church, including the amazing staff members who've worked with me, side by side, to dream about what God could do and then decide together if we have the nerve to do it. Love and laughs have kept us going. I want to thank the Man Cave guys who prayed with me over every next step. To the members and attenders who've let me be a small part of what God is doing in your lives, thank you.

Especially, I'd like to thank my biggest support: my beautiful family. My wife, Karin, is my best friend, confidant, cheerleader, truth teller, and partner for almost a quarter of a century. Without you, there simply is no book, and without you, I probably would never have had the courage to become a pastor. To my daughter,

Katie, and my sons, Jason and Jacob: You three light me up with such joy and laughter, and you constantly remind me of what's at stake with the next generation.

But the biggest thanks is owed to my Lord and Savior, Jesus Christ. He changed the trajectory of my life forever. He saved me, redeemed me, and set my feet on a new path. He gave me a fullness of life I didn't even know was possible. Despite my shortcomings and failures and half-baked motivations, he still decides to use me. May this book glorify him.

Chapter One

THUNDER AND FIRE

Utterly amazed, they asked: "Aren't all these who are speaking Galileans? Then how is it that each of us hears them in our native language? Parthians, Medes and Elamites; residents of Mesopotamia, Judea and Cappadocia, Pontus and Asia, Phrygia and Pamphylia, Egypt and the parts of Libya near Cyrene; visitors from Rome (both Jews and converts to Judaism); Cretans and Arabs—we hear them declaring the wonders of God in our own tongues!" Amazed and perplexed, they asked one another, "What does this mean?"
—ACTS 2:7–12

Imagine being in Jerusalem on *that* day. The city is filled with the exhilarating chaos of thousands of pilgrims preparing for *Shavuot* (the Feast of Weeks). You wake up that morning electric with anticipation. It's a joyous two-day party that celebrates God's blessing on two fronts: Moses receiving the law on Mount Sinai, and the annual wheat harvest. You can't wait for the first fruits presentation at the temple (and the cheers of the crowd) and the smoky sweet fragrance of lamb cooking over the consuming fire. Your mouth is watering just thinking about it.

On this *Shavuot*, you're not only eager to eat, but you're also eager to wash the taste of the last feast out of your mouth. Like most Jews, Passover is usually your favorite. From tasting the *karpas* (bitter herbs) to the *Afikoman* (hidden matzah), it's a meal filled with meaning. It starts in slavery (in Egypt), but by the end of the night, you're set free.[1] But this year, it's different. The whole celebration ends in such disappointment and confusion because of what they did to Jesus.

You remember how the city was buzzing when he showed up. You remember how excited you were. Some of the scribes and teachers were frantically warning people not to listen to him—that he was a false prophet, or worse, a demon. But, truthfully, it only made you want to listen more. And the way he taught. He didn't talk like the others. You had never heard anything like it. It was like a sheep hearing the shepherd's voice: You just wanted to listen.

There are moments from that day—that terrible day—that you just can't get out of your mind. Sometimes, when you close your eyes, you can still hear the sounds. The way the crowd roared with each vicious blow to his body. How he groaned in pain. Nails hammering into the wood. His pleas of thirst. But what you'll never forget—what's burned into your memory forever—are his prayers of forgiveness. Forgiveness not for himself but for the men inflicting the pain. The whole celebration left the taste of *karpas* on your soul. You're ready for some different sounds—joyful sounds.

And then you hear it. It's a low rumble at first, like horses galloping across the Kidron Valley. But it grows louder, more like a powerful windstorm. You look out into the streets. The normally bustling crowd seems frozen in place, ready to either take cover or defend themselves. Everyone's now looking toward a group charging up the street. *Has the celebration begun? Is it a parade?* No, they are shouting something. It sounds like gibberish. *Are they drunk already? It's only nine o'clock in the morning!* But no one is running. They're just . . . listening. Some are nodding their heads like they understand. You think you recognize some Arabic—*or is it Greek?* Some are lifting their hands in praise. As the group comes closer, you can now see and hear a little better. You recognize Hebrew and Aramaic. They are proclaiming God's goodness and mercy—they are shouting his promises! They are reminding us that once we were slaves, but now we are free! *What's going on here? What does this mean?*

It's No Accident

No matter how many times I read or preach on this text, I just can't get my head around what it must have felt like. The thundering power. The shock and confusion. The supernatural transformation of those trembling Jesus followers into thundering Jesus proclaimers. Tongues of fire dancing over their heads, and foreign words feeling familiar across their lips.

It was thunder and fire—the presence of God, just like on Mount Sinai. Except God wasn't just handing his Word *to* the people—God was handing it *through* his people, empowering them to do what only God can do. It was the first gift of the Holy Spirit to the church: the gift of supernatural translation—the wonders of God into the language of the people. I believe it was no accident that it was the first gift, and I believe it points to the fundamental purpose of the church.

Okay, theology nerds: Let's nerd out.

Obviously, the incarnation of Jesus Christ is about atonement. But, in a broader sense, it's about translation. Jesus isn't just a concept (as you know). He's the Incarnate One—the Word that "became flesh and dwelt among us" (John 1:14 ESV). "God with skin on" (as a youth pastor friend used to say). One person, two natures: Jesus of Nazareth *and* the Eternal Logos.

This means that God isn't a conceptual God but a real God, in the sense that God's very nature is voluntarily intertwined with concrete human history. It can be measured and chronicled and interpreted because it's observable. Jesus Christ didn't simply experience the human condition in general; he experienced it specifically through the cultural perspective of first-century Galilee and Roman Judea. From his childhood, he participated in the traditions of Second Temple Judaism: circumcised on the eighth day, schooled in the Scriptures along with his classmates, and trained in obedience to the Law of Moses.

We know that Jesus was baptized, became an itinerant rabbi (with his own unique interpretation of the law), chose disciples, and attended religious festivals in Jerusalem and at least one memorable wedding in Galilee. While the scriptural witness does not explicitly affirm his knowledge of carpentry, tradition would suggest that he knew something of his father's trade. Everything he taught, every person he loved, every miraculous sign he offered, and every argument he engaged in was tethered to his particular first-century culture. In other words, the wonders of God were made known through Jesus Christ into the particular cultural language he lived in.

Okay, we're almost there.

Now, as we know, Jesus's particular culture wasn't and isn't the endgame. The mission is to bring the gospel to every culture. As Jesus said, "You will be my witnesses in Jerusalem, and in all Judea and Samaria, and to the ends of the earth" (Acts 1:8). The incarnation is God's Self-Communication to the world. Jesus claimed, "If you really know me, you will know my Father as well. From now on, you do know him and have seen him" (John 14:7). Incarnation, at its heart, is about translation.

That's why Christianity is so portable across cultures. That's its DNA. For example, we believe there is one true gospel, but there's no one way to express it. You know this from Sunday school. If I'm teaching the story of Job to kindergartners (I don't know why I would—but work with me here), it's going to be expressed much differently than if I were teaching it to teenagers or adults (hopefully). As Tim Keller points out in *Center Church*, "There is no one, single way to express the Christian faith that is universal for everyone in all cultures."[2] Why? Because it will make more sense to some and less to others. Translation is required.

Jesus came so we can see and know the Father. He came to declare the wonders of God in the language of the people. As theologian Andrew Walls puts it, the incarnation is "an act of divine translation par excellence."[3] Jesus calls his church to do the same. His call to go into all the world is a call to gospel translation, to make the Word of God "flesh" for the world to see. Since Pentecost, the thunder and fire flow through us so they may "see [our] good deeds and glorify [our] Father in heaven" (Matt. 5:16). Pentecost reveals (what should be) the primary activity of the church: to translate the never-changing message of Jesus into the ever-changing language of culture. The problem is a vast number of churches in the United States haven't been effectively translating for decades.

Bill's Story

Bill was a teenager growing up in the 1990s. He was a church kid. When he had an opportunity to participate in a mission trip to Germany, he jumped at the chance. Of course, he didn't know much about the mission work, what was being asked of him, or *any* of the German language. But hey, Germany.

He was no stranger to mission trips. He figured it would be like the stateside trips he'd become so familiar with: Show up with a bunch of other youth group kids, stay up late, and maybe paint a few houses. When he arrived, he discovered that there were exactly *two* teenagers participating in this trip: him and a very quiet teenage girl.

Leading the trip was a middle-aged woman who was a taskmaster and whose thick, German accent made her incredibly difficult to understand. On their first day of mission work, this woman (without warning) took them to a local pub in the middle of nowhere. As they opened the door, they saw it was full of farmers and other locals drinking from large steins of beer and sitting in well-worn wooden stools—like churchgoers scattered across the sanctuary in their self-assigned seats.

Again, without warning, the mission leader produced a guitar and told these two teens that they would be singing a worship song for the patrons of the pub. This was their mission work! (At least part of it.) In a blur of nervous confusion, it was decided they would play the classic Paul Baloche tune "Lord, I Lift Your Name on High."

With hands shaking and voices cracking with nerves, they played and sang in English (not German) and ran out of the building as soon as it was over. Bill said that the funny part (now that he had years to heal from this trauma) was that it was like they were completely invisible. No one paid any attention to them. Not even a glance away from their steins. In the end, Bill wasn't convinced the patrons even knew English. They were completely uninspired by the impromptu concert.

Maybe the mission leader pulled this stunt every week, and that's why they didn't pay attention. Or maybe all sorts of musical acts found their way through the doors, and it was just part of the atmosphere (like a jukebox in the background). But a more likely reason is that the song was not only unfamiliar; it was, literally, foreign: simply sung in the wrong language. Believe it or not, this is the same reason many churches in the United States are stuck today: They aren't translating the song (the gospel) into the language of the people. Younger generations especially are both inattentive and uninspired—deaf ears to the good news.

As a result, many (perhaps most) churches that thrived in the 1950s are declining due to their insistence upon continuing with a generational language that largely no longer resonates with the broader culture. These congregations have been too comfortable, terrified, or stubborn to migrate to a different model. They have inadvertently rendered the good news of Jesus Christ into something completely uncompelling to the culture around them.

Lost in Translation

If you're a pastor or church leader, you've heard the bleak news about the state of the church in the United States. The Christian share of the population is shrinking, while the share of atheists, those who practice non-Christian religions, and religiously unaffiliated people ("nones") have all increased dramatically in the last decade. According to the Pew Research Center, "The secularizing shifts evident in American society so far in the twenty-first century show no signs of slowing."[4] I think an especially painful truth is that when people are surveyed about their religious participation, a large majority continue to affirm their belief in God—they just don't believe in church.

As Jake Meador of *The Atlantic* points out: "Forty million Americans have stopped attending church in the past twenty-five years. That's something like 12 percent of the population, and it represents the largest concentrated change in church attendance in American history."[5] In my own denomination, the Presbyterian Church (USA), we lost 709,000 members and 1,557 churches in just ten years (2012–22).[6] This isn't solely because people are becoming less religious. Even regular churchgoers aren't going as much. Whether it's work, youth sports, travel/mobility, or just the felt need to rest on Sundays, even our most committed members are attending less often. At a fundamental level, they find that church is not their most compelling Sunday morning option.

In 2019, *Lifeway Research* reported that 4,500 churches closed their doors forever and that six in ten churches were plateaued or declining. And that was before the COVID-19 pandemic. The pandemic itself was like jet fuel to these declining church trends. In 2022, I was leading a breakout about post-pandemic evangelism at a church conference in Washington, DC. Before my session began, Thom Rainer was leading a breakout in the same room about the post-pandemic church. In that session, he said data from *Lifeway Research* revealed that the pandemic sped up the rate of decline by at least two years. In other words, the attendance decline they saw in 2022 wasn't supposed to happen until 2024.

While recent data suggests a bit of a bounce back for in-person church attendance, many congregations still haven't recovered. In 2023, according to *Lifeway Research*, 67 percent of churches had fewer than one hundred people in worship. And 30 percent had fewer than fifty.[7] Pastors are tired and frustrated and wondering if anything can be done to stop the bleeding. Even more are starting to think that nothing can be done and that their churches will just eventually bleed out.

How is this even possible? How have we turned the gospel—the shocking, overwhelming, beautiful, in-your-face reality of God's never-ending and all-consuming love for us—into something that elicits nothing more than a faint yawn? How is it possible that millions of Americans who live within five minutes of several churches wake up on Sunday morning without so much as a thought about God? Why is cutting grass, sleeping in, travel sports, or pregame NFL programming so much more compelling than Jesus? Because churches have been singing "Lord, I Lift Your Name on High" in German bars.

The church in the 1950s and 1960s was the social hub of society. In the wake of World War II, people joined churches not only because they were the places to meet others in the community but also because church participation became a means of affirming the "American way of life." It was a time when ice cream socials at church also served as business networking opportunities and local political town halls. As religious historians note:

> Mainline Protestant denominations [that] had been stagnant during the 1930s, suffering from the Great Depression and low birth rates . . . [saw] a revival of religion, or at least of an interest in religion, and the era was one that was a comfortable time for the churches . . . at least in terms of seminary enrollments, facility construction, and membership rolls that were bolstered by the baby boom.[8]

Not only were churches exploding with growth, but Christians enjoyed the perks of Christendom: "specially designed privileges for the church in society . . . a dominant culture that bore the deep imprint of Christian values, language, and expectations regarding moral behaviors."[9] In other words, Christians had front row seats to US culture. There was a Christian bias—prayer in schools, wearing your Sunday best, God and country—that was the norm. For example, in 1955, *The Los Angeles Times* had an entire religion section that included celebrity-written devotionals, church news, and an entire page just for Presbyterians. Ah, those were the days.

Over the next seventy years, the way of life in the United States changed in ways that were simply unthinkable in the 1950s and 1960s. The cultural shift between the World War II generation (those born before 1946) and their children (baby boomers) became so dramatic that it led anthropologists like Margaret Mead to use the term "generation gap" to describe the growing cultural dissonance and distance between them.

This cultural language barrier (or gap) has grown with each succeeding generation after the baby boomers. Gen Xers (born 1965–80), millennials (born 1981–96), and Gen Zers (born 1997–2012) have participated less and less in religious activity. For example, according to the Barna Group, a staggering 43 percent of millennials do not believe in God or care that God exists.[10]

It reminds me of Judges 2:10: "After that whole generation had been gathered to their ancestors, another generation grew up who knew neither the Lord nor what he had done for Israel."

This phenomenon is, at its heart, a translation problem. Each generation views church so differently that it's a struggle to find common ground. This is because different generations have such drastically different ways of understanding the world: communication, technology, family dynamics, school, entertainment—basically, everything. Yet, most churches still employ a one-size-fits-all approach. The bias is toward the cultural language of the "builders" (born 1928–45). The dominant cultural language used to communicate the wonders of God to today's young adults (Gen Z) is a gap of five generations.

No wonder they're not in the building.

Let's be clear: I'm not just talking about worship style. I'm talking about the way we typically do church: our traditions, programs, systems, and strategies. This is not a book about worship wars, primarily because the war is over (although some skirmishes persist). Contemporary/modern worship has won (for now). But only until another style takes its place.

Before you throw this book at something expensive, hear what I'm saying: The traditional style (organ, choir, liturgy) can be a wonderful, faithful expression of worship that still resonates with many—just not with many people (statistically speaking) under fifty. It just doesn't move them in the same way. It doesn't open their hearts up to God in the same way. It doesn't mean you need to be happy about it, but it does mean you can't ignore it.

The Problem with Antique Tables

When I was growing up, we had a couple of antique tables that were passed down through the generations. One belonged to my great-grandma Katie. She brought it with her from Austria when she came to the United States in the early 1900s. It was, to my untrained eye, a pretty unremarkable end table.

But no matter where we lived, whether an apartment or a house, the table was always in the hallway. My mom would polish it a couple times a week, and every time I walked by it, I could smell the faint smell of chemical lemons. We were warned never to rest a drink (or anything) on it for fear of damaging it. I distinctly remember the first (and last) time my stepdad put his beer on it. Let's just say he was warned. The table was polished and clean, but in the end, it was unusable because of its significance. It was essentially a museum piece.

Around the time my little sister was born, my Uncle Lou made us a coffee table. It survived many drinks, spills, kids, dogs, and even a move across the country. We loved that table. Eventually, we upgraded to something newer, but nobody wanted to get rid of it. It had so much history. So, we put it in the garage, where it sat for a decade collecting dust and rotting away with the smell of lawn mower gas and engine oil. This table, too, had become unusable.

This is not unlike our historic churches. Often, they become museum pieces or time capsules from a bygone era. *Don't change the service. Don't change the bulletin. Don't change the curtains in the parlor that I hung with my father in 1978. Preserve and protect. Everything is lemony fresh, so don't do anything to damage it.* We not only appreciate the past; we want to live in it.

But museums cost money to maintain. If churches don't have the funds, they often just collect dust from years of neglect. Deferred maintenance. No money. No fresh vision. No risk-taking because church leaders don't want to lose what little they have.

I've heard it said that the biggest threat to your future success is your current success. Why? Because you'll always want to freeze time. In other words, you'll keep doing something the same way because it worked so well once. Ironically, the reason it was successful was probably because it was, at one time, innovative.

No matter which "table" a church has become, it's for the same reason. It's because the gravitational pull is to fossilize around a particular way of doing things. This is completely understandable. But it often leads to a greater disconnect with the culture. Whether a church is like a museum piece or something that smells like a garage, the result is the same: the church is rendered unusable for younger generations. What good are our beloved history and traditions if there's no one to hand them to?

What's the alternative? Should we just do away with all the antique tables? Of course not. Our history matters. Our traditions matter. We just need to become a different kind of table. We need to take all that history and legacy and make it functional—usable—for the next generation. We need to be like reclaimed wood tables. We need to refurbish what we've been to make it both functional and beautiful for this cultural moment.

That's why my friend Jesse Skiffington and I started *The Reclaimed Leader* podcast in 2017. We were trying to lift up this idea of becoming leaders dedicated to effective gospel translation—reclaimed leaders. We knew that we (and other pastors) would need to cultivate the skills, support, and training to help open our congregations to the thunder and fire of God—to reclaim the first gift of the Holy Spirit to the church: translating the wonders of God into the language of the people.

Okay, so how do we do it?

There's a Process

The goal of this book is to equip you with a cultural translation process—the bridge-building blueprints to connect the gospel to your particular culture. It will help you decide what bridges to build, where to build them, and how to plan the construction. The good news? It's not about leadership talent (no offense—I'm sure you're talented). What I mean is that the process *itself* is the talent.

Pastors (and their churches) get stuck around vision. Pastor A sees herself as a visionary. She is an idea factory and never met a brainstorming session she didn't like. She thinks her self-assigned role as visionary in chief means she must go to the mountain and come down with the stone tablets to move her church forward. Pastor B sees himself as a shepherd. He excels at pastoral care but doesn't feel gifted in vision. He has resigned himself to the fact that his church just can't make big changes because he doesn't have big vision.

Both pastors suffer the same problem: They don't understand how leading change works. If you have the right process, it doesn't matter if you're a visionary or not. Vision isn't (primarily) your role. John Kotter, a Harvard professor and expert in leading change, believes that the first step is not for the leader to articulate a vision but to develop a sense of urgency around the problem (which we'll see in Chapter Two).[11]

The process we're going to walk through together, one that will help you lead faithful gospel translation, I call the 4D Process (Discover, Discern, Decide, Deploy). The "Ds" represent distinct strategic stages to help frame the bridge you're going to build. In the Discover stage, you'll identify who you are as a congregation (Chapter Two) and who you're trying to reach (Chapter Three). In the Discern stage, you'll explore how to faithfully develop strategies for gospel translation. Starting with how effective translation happens (Chapter Four), we'll continue by diving deeper into four key translation areas for younger generations: worship (Chapter Five), next gen ministries (Chapter Six), discipleship (Chapter Seven), and evangelism (Chapter Eight). Then, in the Decide stage, you'll finalize the steps to translate and develop a plan of action through key result areas (Chapter Nine). Finally, in Chapters Ten, Eleven, and Twelve, you'll use the Deploy stage to execute and evaluate your translation plan.

The four core stages, or "Ds," are my way of organizing the key revitalization strategies I've learned, along with the foundational insights of Bob Whitesel, honed from his decades of experience as a church consultant and scholar. Baked into the "4Ds" are Kotter's steps for leading successful change, particularly: developing a sense of urgency, creating a guiding coalition, developing a strategic vision, communicating the vision, and recruiting a volunteer army to do it all.[12]

This is the same field-tested, research-based process I've used to help a declining Presbyterian church transform into a flourishing multigenerational (and soon-to-be multisite) congregation. It's the same process I teach (and help lead) with congregations all over the country. I've discovered that it works for big things like crafting an overarching theological vision or smaller, more specific things, like starting a men's ministry for thirtysomethings. It works for small, mid-size, and large churches—because it's not just about what you choose to do but how you do it that determines your success.

Effective gospel translation is not going to happen because of gimmicks or slick programming or dazzling technology. It's going to happen because you engage your church in a prayerful, faithful process of alignment with God's will. If you have the right process, you can become a healthier congregation regardless of size, because it's not just about numerical growth. The number one metric of a healthy process (and the 4D Process) is increased faithfulness to God's mission.

Don't get overwhelmed by all the steps. Just take each one as it comes. Remember, the 4D Process is like a series of steps that start out in darkness and end in light, where you'll uncover God's revitalization plan for your church. If you trust the process, you'll be able to more effectively translate the wonders of God into the language of the people.

A friend of mine told me that in Alcoholics Anonymous, they talk about sobriety in a similar way, by acknowledging that the process works when you work it. That seems to be true with just about everything. Want to write a book? Stick to a daily word goal. Want to lose weight? Stick to the health plan. Want to run faster? Stick to the training. Want to learn biblical Hebrew? Forget it (just kidding)—stick to the course assignments.

As a fellow pastor in the trenches, I know how hard it can be to get forward movement in your congregation. I know you feel a bit helpless sometimes. I know it can be lonely sitting where you're sitting. Sometimes, it feels like you're the only one seeing clearly, the only one who feels burdened by God's mission to the one more than the comfort of the ninety-nine. I know you struggle with self-doubt sometimes (who doesn't?).

But there is good news. What if you aren't as far away from breakthrough as you think? What if everything you hope God will do is still on the table? What if you (yes, you) are exactly the person God wants to use to make a difference? I promise that if you use the tools in this book, it will help your church become healthier.

Are you ready?

For Further Thought: Initial Observations

Let's take a quick snapshot of your church by exploring a few questions.

- You meet someone in the community, and they're curious about your church. How would you describe it to them?
- How would a church member describe your church? Would they talk about its past or its future? Why do you think that is?
- If you approached someone in the neighborhood and asked them to describe your church, what would they say?
- What is the biggest challenge your church is facing right now? What about this challenge makes it so critical?
- What is the biggest opportunity your church has right now? What makes it so important to focus on?

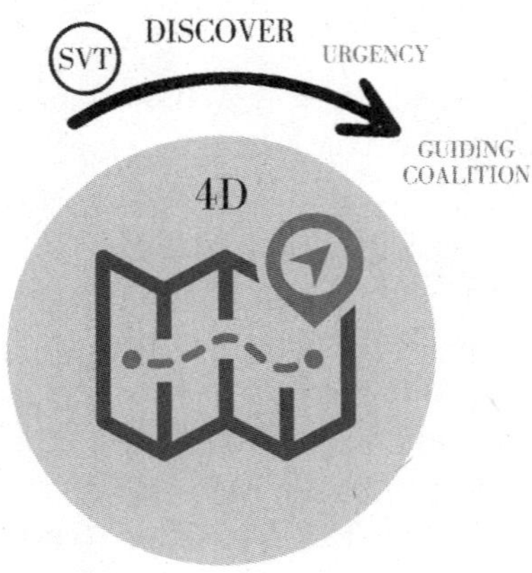

Chapter Two

FACING THE SCALE

Then you will know the truth, and the truth will set you free.
—JOHN 8:32

Tradition is not to preserve the ashes, but to pass on the fire.
—GUSTAV MAHLER

Sheryl Crow once sang "The First Cut Is the Deepest" (originally a Cat Stevens song). Although it's a song about first love (not gospel translation), it still feels like an apt title for the beginning of the 4D Process. That's because the first step always cuts the deepest. This, in part, is because the first step has to do with an honest assessment of who you are as a congregation (we'll get to that in a minute). But I think it's also a confidence thing.

When you're first getting started, you don't know what you don't know. You tend to second-guess a lot. You're not really sure what it's going to take to get across the finish line. There are so many possible targets, you're not certain which one to aim at first. You're thinking, *What if I pick the wrong one? What if we decide to work on Sunday school when we should've started with our volunteer structure? What if we decide to work on launching a new worship service but we should've started with small groups? What if we get our gospel translation wrong? What if? What if? What if?*

Let me put your mind at ease.

How you do it is more important than what you choose to do first (a little louder for the pastors in the back). As long as you pick a relevant ministry goal and align your organization around it, it is the right choice. How can that be? Because regardless of the outcome, it's the act of taking a risk (and trusting God's lead) together that deepens the discipleship of your church. Discipleship is the very thing that's going to make it all work.

After all, the goal of revitalization is faithfulness. Everything else—successful ministry strategies, greater engagement in the life of the church, etc.—is all a byproduct of faithfulness. Revitalization happens when a faith community decides not just to lead change but to lead change in God's direction—a change that begins in the heart and moves to the hands and feet; a change that must necessarily start with the church before it can spread to the culture around it; a change that reawakens hearts for God's mission to the world, helping wayward prodigals and stubborn elder brothers and sisters dine with the Father.

Stage One: Discover

The first step in the process is to discover. If you don't know who you are (identity), your path is unclear (purpose), and it's nearly impossible to move forward. It's like Jason Bourne in *The Bourne Identity*. Suffering a traumatic episode at sea, he survives but has no recollection of who he is—only fragments and dreams that make him anxious, restless, and frenetic. It's lots of sideways energy (and butt-kicking) that has no meaningful direction. Or it's like a college student who hasn't chosen a major—they just don't know what steps to take next. But once they do pick a major, the fog lifts and the path is illuminated.

Church revitalization works in much the same way. Once you discover who you are (identity) and who you're trying to reach (purpose), the fog lifts and the path becomes clearer. Before we go any further, I can already feel the theological side-eye happening: *Wait a minute! We are the church, the body of Christ, and we're trying to reach everyone! We already know our identity and purpose, thank you very much.* Of course, yes, I agree. But, within that framework, we must also ask: *Who are the particular people God is calling us to reach that we are not reaching (and therefore not being faithful to our purpose)? In what ways is our sociological reality helping or hindering our theological or ecclesiological reality? What are the roadblocks that prevent us from carrying out the mission God has called us to?*

Remember, we live in a dual reality—a two-natures reality. Already and not yet. Sinners and saints. Citizens of heaven and citizens of Earth. A theological and sociological community. When I talk about the identity of your church, I'm asking: How is the way you do church, as a sociological reality, maximizing your faithfulness to the mission? How effective are you at translating the wonders of God into the language of the people?

Let's say my church wants to start a new outreach to nearby students at a local university. Let's assume that the congregation currently has no one younger than seventy-five years old. What should we do? First, we have to acknowledge who we are. *What are we good at? What are we not so good at? If we had college students in the building, would we know what to do with them? Is the way we do church helping or hurting our ability to connect?* Then, we have to get to know the students: *What are their hopes, dreams, pain points, baggage about church, and thoughts about Jesus?* Then we can start thinking about strategies to reach them.

It's Going to Take Leadership

As Max De Pree says, "A leader's job is to define reality."[1] Before we get started, let's define what your real leadership role is. I'm willing to bet that your calendar is already full before you start any kind of revitalization process. I'm sure the thought has crossed your mind: *How will I possibly have time to do all this?* Again, let me set your mind at ease.

Leadership does not mean running the entire process. That's management. John Kotter explains:

> Management is a set of processes that can keep a complicated system of people and technology running smoothly . . . Leadership defines what the future should look like, aligns people with that vision, and inspires them to make it happen despite the obstacles . . . successful transformation is 70 to 90 percent leadership and only 10 to 30 percent management.[2]

The pastor's role is to lead—to spark momentum and get the process moving. It's the role of the leadership team to share the heavy lifting of management. If it's your responsibility alone, revitalization won't happen. Or if it does, it certainly won't be sustainable.

Take the NFL, for example. A professional team typically has both a head coach and a general manager. The head coach is in charge of the playbook and the in-game strategies. He's often in the locker room giving speeches, developing relationships with players, and learning how to properly inspire and motivate the team to succeed. The general manager, on the other hand, deals with operations: player acquisitions, contracts, practice locations, team transportation—the business of the franchise.

Every once in a while, an owner of a team will decide to give the coach the authority usually reserved for the general manager, thus conflating the two roles into one. It's usually a disaster because there are just too many demands (and sometimes competing demands) for one person to successfully negotiate both roles at any given time. They can't quite get it to work, no matter how talented and committed (and well-paid) they are.

For this process, you are the "coach." One of the most important first steps you'll take is to select your "general manager." This will be your strategic vision team (SVT). As the coach, you'll focus on strategizing, teaching, and motivating the players to run out of the tunnel, burst through the paper banner, and take the field. Let the strategic vision team share the operational demands so you can do what only you can do. Leading the revitalization process, and the revitalization itself, are both team sports.

The Myth about Vision

Let's continue our talk about vision. Most leaders think that the first step in the revitalization process is for the pastor to supply an awe-inspiring vision—to meet with God on Mount Sinai and return, face aglow, with the stone tablets. Newsflash: it's not. I've learned this the hard way.

Part of the problem is that I am a vision person. I almost always have more ideas in my head than can make it to paper, people, or a process. I'm a dreamer. When I started as a fresh-off-the-line, newly ordained pastor, I thought my big dreams would rally the troops, that my church would be so inspired by my vision that we'd magically have Pentecost excitement and unity. Like I said, I was new.

The result is that I chased dozens of shiny revitalization targets that just made the congregation dizzy. It was like trying to focus on a disco ball. I had vision but no real buy-in from the people. I didn't have a real strategy. I found that instead of inspiring the congregants, I was frustrating them. This was primarily because the church didn't own the vision. They were supplied the vision (or maybe force-fed is more accurate).

If you're a visionary leader, don't worry: your vision will still have a role (probably a major one). But it's not your job to ascend the mountain and receive the vision alone. You need to take your SVT with you (and eventually your congregation) and return with the figurative stone tablets together. Step One is to assemble your team.

You may be wondering: *Is the SVT the same thing as our elder board or governing body?* The short answer is no. Here's why: you don't want to be hamstrung by the polity of your church to decide who sits around the table. As Jim Collins puts it in *Good to Great*, you want to make sure you get "the right people on the bus."[3] Your SVT shouldn't be limited by your organizational chart. You want the people who are the best fit to think and act strategically (see the guidelines at the end of this chapter).

This strategy will keep your leadership movements nimble. Don't worry about your polity. If your polity requires your board to authorize the vision (like mine), the SVT will present its research and recommendations for approval. This ends up being a really good thing in that it generates additional buy-in early. The goal here isn't to bypass their authority; it's to work more efficiently and effectively—speeding up the time it takes to move things forward.

Then, once the SVT is assembled, you'll be ready to start the Discover stage. Since you'll be working on the vision together, your first move will be to get them to see why the vision is necessary. They need to care as much as you do about the need for gospel translation. John Kotter, as mentioned in the previous chapter, teaches that the first step isn't to develop a vision; it's to develop a sense of urgency.[4]

Develop a Sense of Urgency

Urgency around what? What are we going to work on? We haven't even decided what needs to change. It's okay; we'll get there. Eventually, you'll develop urgency for your congregation around the ministry initiatives your team will develop (but that comes later). At first, you simply need to develop urgency within the team itself. You need to help them see what you see and feel what you feel. Understand that if they don't figure things out now, there are very real consequences.

Status quo is stronger than you think. Remember the antique tables. It takes a lot of convincing to decide to refurbish (change what's always been) for the sake of usability for the next generation. Even if everyone agrees that it's necessary. "Establishing a sense of urgency is crucial to gaining needed cooperation. With complacency high, transformations usually go nowhere because few people are even interested in working on the problem."[5] The gravitational pull of just about every church that's been around a while is to talk about it, think about it, but not do anything about it. This takes a lot of energy to change, and it's why many pastors don't even try. But the consequences of not trying are catastrophic.

When Status Quo Rules

A few years ago (pre-pandemic), I was part of a team that was leading a youth mission trip to Schenectady, New York. The students, from church youth groups all across the country, were scheduled to arrive on Sunday afternoon. The staff, however, were required to arrive the night before. Our custom was to find a church to attend on Sunday morning before the students showed up. I'm not sure how we decided on which church to go to, but I suspect it had to do with the convenience of the worship time.

The church we picked that Sunday was a beautiful stone structure from the late 1800s with good parking (pastors, you get it). The outside edifice looked well-maintained. The plants had a fresh layer of dark brown mulch, and the grass was meticulously manicured. The inside, however, told a different story. Our group (about ten of us) walked through the front entryway into a large, squarish room with a high, vaulted ceiling. Maybe three or four people (who looked about seventy years old) were gathered around a large metal coffee urn on a foldable card table and sipping from white paper cups. Another was sitting on a leather couch with what looked like a homemade, multicolored afghan blanket draped over it. An eclectic mix of chairs were positioned in a kind of oval around an area rug. It looked like someone was trying to create a living room vibe but, to be honest, it looked more like a garage sale.

It wasn't dirty; it was just dated. It was hard to escape the feeling that I had just entered my grandma's house after school in second grade. The only things missing were the plastic covers on the furniture and a giant Zenith television playing reruns of *Mash*. I was snapped back to attention, however, when a finely dressed man handed us bulletins and led us down a hallway to the sanctuary.

As I entered the sanctuary, it was exactly as I expected. It had a long, red-carpeted aisle down the middle, flanked by symmetrical wooden pews. Red hymnals and black, hardcover Bibles were in racks. Two sets of yellowish stained-glass windows were on each side. In the front were a traditional wooden lectern, pulpit, and communion table. There was a US flag on one side and a Christian flag (*by the way, who decided that flag?*) on the other. It was basically a carbon copy of most of the historic denominational sanctuaries in the Northeast.

Greg Atkinson is a church consultant and an expert in church first impressions. When he was a guest on *The Reclaimed Leader* podcast, he explained that first-time guests (according to research) make up their minds about whether they're coming back in the first seven minutes. In this case, I only needed three.

There were maybe ten to fifteen congregants scattered across the sanctuary (our group effectively doubled the attendance). We brought the average age down by probably forty years (no exaggeration). Some looked up and smiled at our arrival. An organist was playing some prelude music, but it didn't seem like anyone was really listening—they just gazed at their bulletins. There was no energy. Actually, it was an energy drain. I know this was a me problem, but I was looking forward to the end before it even started.

As worship began, I started looking ahead in the bulletin to (you know) measure the length of the journey. The thing that caught my eye immediately was that a children's message was planned (there weren't even middle-aged people, let alone kids). I started to wonder how the pastor was going to handle it. *Will he laugh it off? Or will he ignore it and move on to the next thing without skipping a beat? Will he use it as an opportunity to encourage the congregation to invite their grandkids?*

He didn't do any of those things.

When the children's message came, he did the one thing I didn't see coming: he gave the message anyway. When he first started, I thought he was kidding. I even let out a small laugh (true story). But this was no joke. He was fully committed to delivering the children's message with no children in the room. If he shortened the message, the original must've been a doozy, because he went on for about ten minutes. It did not count as his sermon. He did that too.

After the service, I wanted to ask about the children's message. I had so many questions. But as I approached him back near the coffee urn, I could see he was elated by the larger-than-usual crowd, and I didn't want to bring him down. I asked one of the members (a friendly looking woman who was probably about eighty years old) as we drank from our white paper cups: "Do you usually get many children for the children's message?"

"No," she said. "Maybe once or twice a year we have some families that come visit from out of town."

"Does the pastor always give the children's message?" I asked.

"Oh yes!" she replied. "Don't tell him, but we like the children's message better than the sermon!"

There was a lot more I wanted to ask, but I decided to leave it alone. Although this is an amusing memory, it is no joke. It's a microcosm of the problem happening with churches all across the country: Younger generations have slipped away because we have become tone-deaf to their needs. We've insisted on preserving our traditions instead of seeking to connect. We've refused to translate the wonders of God into the language of the people.

The Power of Urgency

Are churches like this incapable of adapting? Are they simply too far gone? I'm not buying it. Why? Because the proof is in the pandemic. According to *Lifeway Research*, prior to the COVID-19 pandemic, a large number of Protestant pastors indicated that they didn't utilize any online worship options. However,

> As the coronavirus began to spread and social distancing guidelines emerged, the vast majority of churches quickly provided digital options. By March 2020, Lifeway Research found 92 percent of Protestant pastors said they provided some type of video sermons or worship services online. That climbed to 97 percent in April 2020.[6]

That's the power of urgency. It pushes through the obstacles. Most churches (including that church in Schenectady) found a way to offer online worship. Some small churches used Zoom. Some stuck an iPhone in the back of the room and recorded or streamed to Facebook. Churches that hadn't made any significant change in decades found a way to make it happen—fast. How do you create a sense of urgency without needing a global pandemic? You start by facing the scale.

I've struggled with weight my whole life. I was an offensive lineman in high school. Lifting weights, getting stronger, putting on muscle—it all came easy because of my body type. But eventually, those testosterone-fueled, high-intensity exercise years subsided. Thus, I have a love–hate relationship with the scale. Mostly hate.

The toughest time is between Thanksgiving and New Year's Day. That timespan is when I tend to eat, drink, and be merry. But merriment comes at a cost. I procrastinate when it comes to stepping on the scale to assess the damage. Here's a question: The longer I put it off, do you think the number on the scale gets better or worse? Worse? Why? Because until I face the pain, I won't feel the urgency to make a change. You can't address what you're unwilling to assess. According to a 2022 article about weight loss, the "evidence suggests that people who regularly weigh themselves are more likely to lose weight and keep it off than those who don't."[7] Why? Because it destroys ambivalence: "the emotion that's standing in the way of your healthy change."[8]

If you've ever watched *Restaurant Impossible*, starring chef Robert Irvine, you can see him utilize this tactic beautifully (and a little brutally). In the show, Irvine visits failing restaurants and promises to give them the tools they need to turn around—including a restaurant makeover—in only two days and with a budget of ten thousand dollars. On the first day, he tastes the food (and usually spits it out dramatically), checks the sanitary conditions (which are always disgusting), and interviews staff (who are always desperate). When he presents his findings to the owners and tells them how bad it is, the same reactions occur: anger, defensiveness, and defiance.

But what Irvine knows is that unless the owners face the scale and see how bad the damage is, they'll never change. The status quo is just too strong, even for a business that is failing (often losing hundreds of dollars a day). Did you catch that? Even a business that knows it needs help will resist that help. This is what makes church renewal so difficult. Not because church members act like the owners (although they do) but because pastors are the ones who get defensive and angry—so much so that they'd rather not face the scale at all.

We, too, must destroy ambivalence. It sounds simple, but facing the scale is perhaps the hardest step (especially for pastors) to take. Why? Because it's painful. Many pastors feel it's an indictment on their leadership (it's usually not, but it feels that way). They see the numbers and offer excuses. They deflect. Whenever I do a church consultation, this is the hardest part. The first cut is the deepest, but it may be the most important.

The first cut reveals the truth. It doesn't just address the symptoms; it gets to the underlying causes. The check-engine light of your church has been on for a while, but you don't know how bad it is until you open the hood. It's a vulnerable, sometimes embarrassing, and often frustrating endeavor. But again, you can't fix what you're unwilling to acknowledge. Facing the scale is what no pastor really wants but what every pastor needs.

I heard somewhere that you can either make progress or make excuses, but you can't do both. I believe that's true. Facing the scale creates the urgency to make a change. When you see how much weight you've gained (so to speak), then you discern what health strategies are available, decide which strategy to try, and decide when to start. If all of us can get past the defensiveness and fears of failure and remind ourselves of the urgency of God's mission, we can move forward.

How Do I Face the Scale?

Facing the scale is about discovering your identity (think Jason Bourne). It's about getting your church to answer the questions: *Who are we really? Who are we right now?* (As opposed to who your church was in the past.) This should be an honest self-assessment. By asking some key questions and collecting necessary data, you'll start to paint a picture of the current state of your church. Until you do this, you'll never really understand the gaps preventing you from effective gospel translation.

To get started, set up an SVT meeting. Explain that, to address the urgent ministry challenge your church is facing, you'll need to gather data to properly assess the current health of your church. But you're not just collecting information.

You're also spending time on interpretation. To do that, you'll ask four questions (each with their own built-in steps): *What are the numbers saying? What are the people saying? What is our Sunday morning experience saying? Where are we in the life cycle?* Before we unpack these a bit more, let me offer a tip and a warning.

First, it will be important that, as you collect data, you delegate to the SVT as much as possible. For example, if looking at church metrics, have one person look at attendance, one look at giving, and so on, and have everyone report back to the group. This whole process has a free Google Docs template available that you can use to plug in your information. You can download it at www.reclaimedleader.com/translation.

Second, a word of warning (and encouragement): This is the most time-consuming part of the Discover stage, as well as the entire process. Don't rush. Urgency isn't about just about speed; it's about resolve. Take your time. Don't skip steps. The prescription is only as good as the diagnosis.

Step One: What Are the Numbers Saying?

In this initial stage, you will start by measuring everything you can measure. What are the metrics for your church over the last five years? (I would omit 2020 because the numbers won't be very helpful—everything was out of whack due to the COVID-19 pandemic.) Some key metrics are: attendance (worship, Sunday school, Bible studies, events), giving, membership (gains and losses), number of baptisms, confirmation students—everything you can measure.

Another source of information is a paid data service like MissionInsite. Check and see if your denomination has a subscription. What they can do is give you community data such as how many new people are moving into a community and their average age, income, marital status, etc. If you want to reach new young families, for example, but no young families live within twenty miles of the church, that's a problem you need to know about.

Step Two: What Are People Saying?

In this step, you'll discover what your congregation believes about who they are. This is a key step. You'll want to know what your own people see as the strengths and weaknesses of your church and the challenges it faces. They may not be accurate assessments. For example, a church member can say that a strength is your youth handbell program that hasn't existed since 1985, but it's their perception you'll need to know how to build consensus as you make changes.

You may want to give your congregation a survey. The more input you can gather, the better. Ask what they see as the top three strengths, the top three weaknesses (or areas of improvement, if that sounds a little better), and the top three future ministry opportunities. As part of the survey, make sure you ask them how long they've been at the church and what roles they have served. This will help you figure out how different demographics (generations) think.

Next, you'll want to convene four focus group sessions. You'll be tempted to skip this step, but I promise it is crucial to your success. Each group will need five to eight participants. They will meet independently of one another, and they can do so over a series of consecutive Sundays or at a one-day event. Group A will be longtime members. Group B will be newer members who have arrived in the last five years. Group C will be your leadership (again, the elders or governance team). Group D will be staff (if applicable).

You will ask them the same questions as the survey: *What are the biggest strengths, weaknesses, and ministry opportunities?* You'll take forty-five minutes for each group. Depending on your church size and dynamics, it may be good to have someone other than you (the pastor) lead these conversations. It's better if the pastor is not in the room for any of these discussions. This is to secure the most honest responses possible. You can have an SVT member or even a trusted ministry colleague at another church lead these focus groups.

Last, ask your team to reach out to neighbors, friends, local business owners, etc., to find out how outsiders view your church.

Have them ask one question: *What do you think of_____church?* They may say, "Never heard of it," "I know someone who goes there," or "My mother used to go there." Listen for any clues about how they perceive the church. Some of the most useful data comes from these conversations, which also build relationships for future potential outreach.

Step Three: What Is Our Sunday Morning Experience Saying?

Next, you'll evaluate your worship service(s), both in person and online. This is one of the most valuable exercises that I do for churches. But you don't need to pay my fee—you can bring in a friend or a pastor whom you trust to give you a good, accurate assessment. *Secrets of a Secret Shopper* by Greg Atkinson does an excellent job detailing some of the things to pay attention to—things like (for in-person services): *Was it easy to find parking? Was I greeted at the door? Did I know where to go or bring my kids? Was there good signage? Was the worship experience engaging? Was the first fifteen minutes all announcements that didn't include me? Was the sermon too long? Did my kids like the Sunday school? Were the environments clean, or did they look like they'd been neglected? Did I feel like I heard from the Lord?* And online: *Was the service easy to find? Was the sound quality good? Did it keep me engaged? Did someone notice I was there?*

Then, after gathering all of this input data (steps one to three), your leadership team will assess where you are in the life cycle of your church—the current vitality and viability of your congregation. Yes, this is the pain point—the final number on the scale. It's the hardest part, but it's the key to destroying ambivalence and taking necessary action.

Step Four: Where Are We in the Life Cycle?

In Les McKeown's book *Predictable Success*, he explains the truth about organizational dynamics through a life cycle diagram.

McKeown argues that every business must be aware of these stages (*early struggle*, *fun*, *whitewater*, *predictable success*, *treadmill*, *big rut*, and *death rattle*) to achieve optimal organizational health (Figure 2.1).[9]

Although his book is written with businesses in mind, it's a helpful tool for understanding the life cycle of churches. In fact, in his book *The Unstuck Church*, Tony Morgan adapts McKeown's model to language around church health (*launch*, *momentum growth*, *strategic growth*, *sustained health*, *maintenance*, *preservation*, and *life support*).[10]

While I highly recommend going through Morgan's book as a resource, here's the upshot: In the upward slope, or the growth edge, of the life cycle, it takes vision to launch and grow. These stages feature creativity, energy, and innovation. For many churches, they are stuck because visionary leadership is absent. And often, it's the reinfusion of vision that helps revitalization efforts get off the ground.

If this upward-moving vision is successful, a natural tension will develop between continued growth and the need for proper systems to maintain it. For McKeown, this is represented in the *whitewater stage* (or *strategic growth* for Morgan). As the organization increases in complexity, there will need to be a higher level of strategic thinking. This is when visionary leaders must invite process leaders to the table. If they don't, the business/church will not continue its upward trajectory. It's only when both visionaries and processors are in alignment that *predictable success/sustained health* is possible.

Some would argue that this is all a bit too business-y. That it's not considering the supernatural reality of the local church. I disagree. In fact, I would argue that on the day of Pentecost, the reason the Holy Spirit came upon them at the same time was because they had obeyed Jesus's parting words: "Do not leave Jerusalem, but wait for the gift my Father promised" (Acts 1:4). In other words, they *organized* themselves, strategically, based on Jesus's command. And because they did, "When the day of Pentecost came, they were all together in one place" (Acts 2:1). It was a partnership between the sociological and the supernatural.

They did what they could do so God could do what only God can do. That's the Church.

Of course, the life cycle also has a downward slope. This is because, over time, even the healthiest organizations tend to fossilize around methods that once worked but no longer make sense (as we saw in Schenectady). When this happens, it's because the visionary leaders have taken a step back and the process leaders have taken control. If this continues without intervention, visionary leaders will become frustrated and move on for other ventures. And the group or church eventually ends in a *death rattle*, or *life support*, unless a new vision is launched.

According to Figure 2.1, where do you place your church in the life cycle? It's okay—facing the scale will tell you the truth, and truth will generate urgency. It will show you the current gaps and future trends. Are you overrun with processors? Are you lacking any visionary leaders? What will happen if you don't address this in the next three years? What if you ignore the numbers and let the status quo continue? What is the opportunity cost of doing nothing? Will the number on the scale get better or worse?

Now Is When It Gets Better

Once you get through this part, it starts to get exciting. You have your SVT (remember, coach and general manager working together), your overall assessment, and a firm grasp of who you are (identity). Now, you're ready to shift your focus to the last question of the Discover stage: *Who is God calling you to reach?*

Guidelines for Selecting Your Strategic Vision Team (SVT)

- Aim for five to eight members.
- They must be team players and work well with others. If they've been difficult in the past, you don't want them on the team—you will still invite their input, but not yet.
- They represent stakeholders. It's helpful if they are generationally diverse and can eventually speak the vision to their tribes.

- They are people who are involved. This team isn't an outreach; you want committed members.
- They are strategic thinkers. It's good to have vision more than process at this point.
- They believe faithfulness to God's mission is everything. You want mature Christians but not stuck Christians—they need to want revitalization for the sake of the gospel.

Figure 2.1. Les McKeown's *Predictable Success*[11]

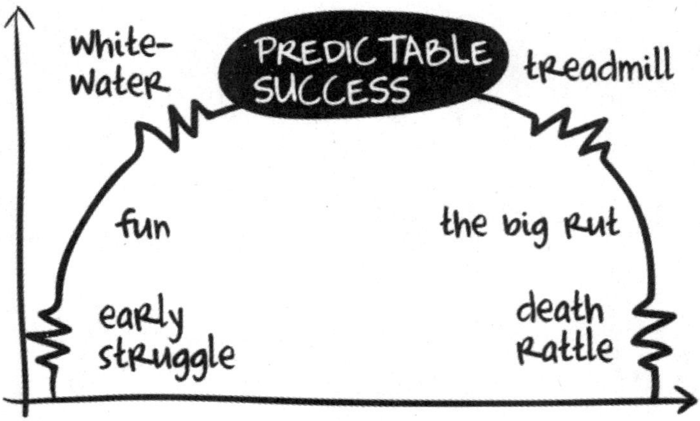

Chapter Three

WHO ARE YOU TRYING TO REACH?

People were bringing little children to Jesus for him to place his hands on them, but the disciples rebuked them. When Jesus saw this, he was indignant. He said to them, "Let the little children come to me, and do not hinder them, for the kingdom of God belongs to such as these. Truly I tell you, anyone who will not receive the kingdom of God like a little child will never enter it." And he took the children in his arms, placed his hands on them and blessed them.

—MARK 10:13–16

On January 1, 2025, media outlets like *Newsweek* and *USA Today* announced that Gen Beta, "the world's youngest generation," [1] had officially arrived. "Mark McCrindle, a demographer and social analyst . . . who previously coined the name Gen Alpha," indicated that this "new generation will span from 2025 until 2039."[2] This generation will be the first to grow up in a world where artificial intelligence is, simply, a part of daily life. That means the church at this moment in history has seven living generations in it. Seven. I can't think of any other institution where this is true.

Theoretically, a churchgoer born in 1925 could be sitting in a pew with a baby born in 2025—a hundred-year span. In 1925, the first television system was tested. In 2025, we can digitally stream thousands of titles anywhere we have cell phone connectivity. Reaching younger generations is going to take some serious translation; but before the translative work can happen, we have to understand what the generational language barriers are.

This brings us to the next step in the Discover stage. Now that you've spent time assessing who you are (identity) as a congregation, it's time to turn your attention to who you're trying to reach (purpose). Why? Because if you don't, you'll end up wasting energy, resources, and perhaps more importantly, time (which leads to poor gospel translation and, quite possibly, a failed mission). Each generational culture is so different that the strategies must be determined by which of the seven you're trying to reach with the gospel. Otherwise, it's like singing English in a German bar.

We Need a New Bias

As we discussed in the first two chapters, our churches in the United States (especially mainline denominational churches) are biased toward older generations ("builders" and boomers) who resonate with a more traditional church experience (again, not just in worship, but in the way to do church). Of course, it's no one's fault that older generations have certain religious preferences; that's true of all generations. "Like it or not, when you were born dictates the culture you will experience . . . . The society that molds you when you are young stays with you the rest of your life."[3]

When I use the term "older generations," let's be clear: I mean Christians who've been shaped by and prefer a post-World War II, traditional church experience. It's a mentality even more than an age. Yes, most of these Christians were born between 1928 and 1964, but there are certainly younger generational outliers. The problem, however, isn't their preferences. It's when they insist that their way is the only way to do church. Research tells us that younger generations "will avoid a church that primarily offers programs and ministries geared to another generation."[4]

That being said, I've never met an older church member (or a more traditional younger member) who didn't long to see younger generations engage in the life of the church. In fact, they absolutely crave it. The problem is when they dictate the terms: *You must appreciate real music—classical choir music that lifts the soul. You need to learn to navigate the hymnal. Your children must attend Sunday school and join the children's choir—and if sports interfere, you must quit them. Your kids should also be in worship, but they must remain silent, especially during a thirty-minute sermon written for us. You must do all the things we did as we raised our families. Of course, you are free to enjoy all the things you enjoy, just so long as it's also the way we enjoy them. And if you don't, maybe your priorities need realigning.*

Maybe that's a little harsh (or even unfair). Certainly, not everyone feels this way or would even say it like this. But this is the message that younger generations are hearing (whether intentionally or unintentionally): *It's our way or the highway.* Our churches need a new bias. Why? Because, as Bob Whitesel and Kent Hunter put it in *A House Divided*:

> Every congregation is in a generational relay and must prepare for an eventual passing of the baton of leadership to a successive generation. . . . Our observation is that the leading reason churches are declining is because most are staffed, programmed, and envisioned to reach one generation.[5]

We've been dancing around this for two chapters, but this is where the music stops: The number one priority of our churches should be to reach younger generations for Jesus Christ. Why? Because we've fumbled the baton. We've failed to engage them with the gospel. Our once-thriving communities of faith have become museums, paying homage to an era long since passed.

Maybe you want to push back against that. I get it. Even in my own church, where we've successfully grown younger, every so often someone will say something like: *But what about nurturing the faith of older generations? What are we doing for them? Aren't they part of our mission, too?* Yes, of course they are. But I honestly believe the best catalyst for spiritual growth of older generations is to actively disciple younger generations.

First, we're already catering to older generations in the way we do church. Second, I don't think another potluck, bus trip, or classical concert is going to grow the faith of a longtime Christian.

It's not that these things are bad—they just aren't faith catalysts. Why? Because a lack of fellowship events is rarely the barrier to spiritual growth. The problem is a deficient understanding of discipleship itself.

Many (if not most) "builder" and boomer Christians in mainline denominations see discipleship as a combination of faithful attendance and volunteerism (the latter they don't do as much because they see it as, ironically, the next generation's turn). They tend to think growing closer to Jesus is primarily about knowledge (Bible studies, theology classes).

But we know that discipleship isn't just about knowledge (we'll dive deeper into this in Chapter Seven). It's not simply a linear, tiered class schedule: Bible 101, 201, 301, etc. It's an apprenticeship. Apprentices learn so they can go do. Whether you're a plumber, a doctor, or a Jedi Padawan, learning comes primarily by doing.

It's like changing a flat tire. When I first got my driver's license, one of my stepdad's pre-driving requirements was to learn this important skill. Of course, I thought this was a complete waste of time because I was sixteen and already knew everything. As he opened the trunk and took the lug wrench, jack, and spare tire out of their hidden compartments, I listened with all the enthusiasm of a dental patient. He talked through each step as he did it, but all I heard was the adult voice that characters in the Charlie Brown cartoons heard. I just kind of rolled my eyes and kept saying, "yes, dad," "uh-huh," and "I know." Except I didn't know, which became painfully clear when I had a flat tire months later. I remembered nothing and had to ask my friend's dad for help.

Learning is cemented by doing. After all, "Faith by itself, if it is not accompanied by action, is dead" (James 2:17). It's like diet and exercise. It's not enough to know about it; you need to do it. The best thing we can do for older or more traditional generations is to empower them to reach and disciple younger generations. When they do, they grow deeper in their faith.

Theologian John Piper, while preaching at the Passion Conference in 2000, delivered a sermon that captured this idea. It's an exhortation not to waste your life:

> I tell you what a tragedy is. I'll read to you from *Reader's Digest* what a tragedy is. "Bob and Penny took early retirement from their jobs in the Northeast five years ago when he was fifty-nine and she was fifty-one. Now they live in Punta Gorda, Florida, where they cruise on their thirty-foot trawler, play softball and collect shells." *That's* a tragedy. And people today are spending billions of dollars to persuade you to embrace that tragic dream. And I get forty minutes to plead with you: don't buy it. With all my heart I plead with you: don't buy that dream. The American dream: a nice house, a nice car, a nice job, a nice family, a nice retirement, collecting shells as the last chapter before you stand before the creator of the universe to give an account of what you did: "Here it is Lord—*my shell collection!* And I've got a nice swing, and look at my boat!" Don't waste your life; don't waste it.[6]

What about nurturing the faith of older generations? What are we doing for them? We're exhorting them not to waste their lives. We're helping them grow by empowering them to perform a successful generational faith handoff as a first-order faith priority.

Do Not Hinder Them

Everyone in Jesus's orbit had an agenda. The teachers of the law, the disciples, the crowd—they all had certain needs they wanted him to meet. Clearly, none of their agendas included stopping to pay attention to the children. Not only did he stop, but in Mark's Gospel, he seemed to prioritize children with his final ministry moments outside the walls of Jerusalem.

After driving out an impure spirit from a young boy (Mark 9:14–29), Jesus and his disciples begin their final journey toward Jerusalem. Apparently, there was some arguing within the disciples' ranks (Mark 9:33), and, ironically, rank was the topic. To settle the matter, Jesus took a child into his arms and said, "Whoever welcomes one of these little children in my name welcomes me" (Mark 9:37). Although his next thoughts can be expanded to include all those who believe, verse 42 feels like an exclamation mark for verse 37: "If anyone causes one of these little ones . . . to stumble, it would be better for them if a large millstone were hung around their neck and they were thrown into the sea." Then in chapter 10, a few verses later, Jesus blessed the children (despite the disciples' initial attempt to make them go away because Jesus supposedly had more important priorities).

Let's put this into perspective. Jesus was on his way to Jerusalem for what he knew would be the final act of his life this side of the cross. This was the last handful of opportunities he would have to teach, connect with, or even come in contact with people outside the walls of the city until they dragged him to Golgotha. In those critical moments, what did he do? He emphasized the faith of children.

The takeaway isn't just Jesus's desire to bless them; it's his admonition not to hinder them. I believe that by refusing to change our mono-generational language of church, we've done exactly that. We've been hindering them because we aren't considering their needs, wants, pain points, or longings. As a result, we've largely failed to translate the wonders of God into their language.

For Me, It's Personal

My childhood was, let's say, a mixed bag. But one thing's for sure: that bag didn't include church. Interestingly, I always believed there was a God (nobody taught me; I just believed it), but I had no idea who God was. Then, in 1992, when I was a nineteen-year-old college student, God made himself known to me.

I was at that stage in life of dancing between complete helplessness and know-it-all arrogance. The truth was, my lifelong dream of becoming a doctor was fading before my organic chemistry goggles, and I was utterly lost. When neither studying hard nor partying harder successfully numbed the pain, I became more and more withdrawn, angry, and depressed.

It was the summer after my freshman year at Allegheny College. After I came home, it didn't take long for me to want to get out of the house. So I looked for a summer job. I grabbed a Sunday edition of the *Pocono Record* (our local paper) and saw an open camp counselor position at Kirkwood Camp and Conference Center across town in Stroudsburg, Pennsylvania. I remember thinking: *I'll get out of the house, have room and board, and play with a bunch of ten-year-olds. How hard could that be?* (I had no idea.)

It was late at night on the third day of staff training. While sitting around a campfire under the stars, I was presented with the gospel, in my language: who Jesus is and what he did on the cross. When I heard it, I just knew it was true. I don't know why; I just knew it. It was the truest thing I ever heard. When a friend, Craig, offered for me to receive Jesus as my Lord and Savior, I didn't hesitate. In June 1992, I became a follower of Jesus Christ.

I often describe my journey of faith as a kind of backwards process. Many (if not most) people learn about Jesus, the Bible, and church before coming to faith. But I didn't really know any of it. I'd never even opened a Bible! When it came to church, I really had no other experience than camp. This proved to be a big challenge to my young faith. This is why thinking about who you're trying to reach is critically important.

My camp experience was incredible. But in a way, it didn't prepare me for the reality of church after camp. When I worshiped in all my new-Christian fervor, it was to acoustic guitars, hand drums, and handclaps. It was full of life, fun, and emotional power (and this was a Presbyterian camp). The loving and caring environment was always so full of anticipation: *God meets me here.*

When camp ended and I returned to Allegheny College, I carried that expectation and anticipation through the doors of several churches, searching to keep my faith from floundering in the midst of my back-to-school reality. Figuring I was a Presbyterian (just based on the camp affiliation), I tried a bunch of Presbyterian churches. Let's just say, whatever my camp experience of Christian community, worship, and discipleship was, these new church experiences were the opposite.

Every church I visited was so stoic, buttoned-up, and emotionless (probably not to the people there, but to me), it felt like I was attending funeral services. Gone was the joy around the campfire. Gone was the anticipation of God's presence. Gone was anyone else my age (even in a college town). In fairness, maybe camp gave me an unrealistic or even deficient expectation of church, which is much more than a feeling. But I wasn't mature enough to understand that. I still needed to be nurtured.

I was hindered in finding Jesus. Of course, nobody meant for that to happen. It wasn't like I didn't feel welcomed into each church I entered. If anything, when I would show up, it was like the church would smell blood in the water and practically shark-attack me with attention. I remember one church invited me to lead its Vacation Bible School (after meeting the pastor for the first time after service)—yikes. The problem wasn't that I was ignored. The problem, largely, was that there was a generational language barrier that they had no interest in fixing.

For example, I needed a worship experience that kept the fire burning. An experience that spoke my language, that could draw me into God. But the worship services I attended simply weren't designed for me, so I moved on to the next. And then the next. But no matter where I went, the "antique tables" were just too unusable.

The Multigenerational Church

If we're going to shake up the status quo, we need to push ourselves to reach younger folks. To start, we need to familiarize ourselves with each generation (see Figure 3.1). While the chart isn't intended to provide a comprehensive analysis of each unique generational language, it can serve as a primer for understanding the barriers. A deeper dive will eventually be necessary. Research will be a critical part of the translation process for your church. After all, how can you translate the gospel if you don't know the language you're translating it to? There are some great, in-depth resources on generational differences (a few are recommended at the end of this chapter).

Let's begin by asking a hypothetical question. Pretend (like many young Americans) that you've never been inside a church sanctuary. To learn about it, you gather five generational representatives (since the sixth and seventh are a bit too young) to answer: *What does a church sanctuary look like?* Their descriptions will help us understand some important differences in generational values. Let's start with the "builders" (1928–45).

How would a "builder" describe a sanctuary? They might talk about stained glass, fine woodwork, wooden pews, and exposed organ pipes. "Influenced by Northern European heritage and art, they often honor God with the craftsmanship of their hands. Thus, their churches tend to be architectural and aesthetic masterpieces . . ."[7] Everything is symmetrical and formal—the chancel flanked by both a US flag and a Christian flag: God and country. It's the sanctuary most of us would see if we randomly walked into a mainline denominational church on a Sunday morning.

Now, the baby boomers (1946–64). They are the children of the 1960s who, generally, were "less religiously active than their parents and grandparents, [and who] lost confidence in the denominations in which they were raised."[8] While many mainline traditional churches are filled with boomers (who still resonate with the traditional church style of their childhood), as a generation, they largely left their parents' version of church.

For many, their biggest religious influence was the Jesus Movement of the 1960s. Think folk music: guitars, tambourines, and bongo drums playing at beach baptisms in Southern California. From this movement, you can draw a direct line to modern contemporary worship. Boomers are largely responsible for the megachurch experience we see today—not just in style but in organization (the transfer of corporate leadership principles to the church).

How would a contemporary-leaning boomer answer the question? They might say that a sanctuary has theater-style seating or comfortable chairs (no more wooden pews) and dramatic lighting and is meant to be more come-as-you-are casual (no more Sunday best). Gone are the formal accoutrements, organ pipes, and choir lofts of their parents' version of church, as they prefer the *auditorium* over the *sanctuary*.

Next is the children of boomers, Generation X (1965–80). The boomers came up with this generational label based on what they were noticing in their kids. "The 'X' was meant to refer to a nihilistic attitude [they] noticed across the widening generation gap."[9] Of course, Gen Xers weren't really as nihilistic as their parents believed. But they were right about the widening gap. Except this gap was more technological than theological.

They were known as the latchkey kids[10] because, for the first time in larger numbers, both parents worked outside the home. They were raised in front of (or sometimes by) television screens. As cable television entered their homes, "There were now over 30 TV channels that could be watched in the home instead of around a measly four."[11] As a result, Gen Xers became TV junkies. They listened to music on it (MTV). They recorded and watched it asynchronously for the first time (through VHS cassettes). Combined with the exponentially higher sound fidelity of CDs (compact discs), Gen Xers became sophisticated audiovisual consumers (and visual learners).

How would they describe a sanctuary? Since they "prefer rapid and colorful presentations [à la MTV],"[12] a Gen Xer will see video projection (screens, TVs) and high-fidelity sound as an integral part of sanctuary design. But unlike their parents, Gen Xers are leery about the church service as a stage production, or show. They have a burning desire for authenticity and intimacy.[13] Therefore, any production elements (lighting, video, music) must be used in service of an authentic, vulnerable experience. It's like scaling the warmth of a campfire through audiovisual kindling, making the auditorium feel smaller and more intimate.

Also referred to as Generation Y, the millennials (1981–96) are so named for their coming of age around the change of the millennium. They're the Internet, or digital, generation. For them, the world got both smaller (more accessible) and bigger (more globally minded). If they had a mantra, it might be something like "life is a cafeteria."[14] This is because their worldview is assembled piecemeal by cherry-picking their favorite cultural and religious expressions. A lot of ink has been spilled over the latter.

The term "nones" (from "none of the above") was coined after a "[2012] Pew Research poll found that the number of Americans who [were] religiously unaffiliated rose to almost 20 percent,"[15] a large number of whom were millennials. The irony is that as teenagers in the 1990s and early 2000s, they were the ones packed into church youth rooms. Some would say their generation was the last big heyday of church youth groups in the United States, maybe because there were so many of them (a staggering nineteen million[16] larger than the boomers).

What happened? Why did they walk away from church? As a Gen X youth minister (and sibling of two millennials), I got to see this generation grow up. In my over twenty years of youth ministry, I saw their religious activity firsthand. I saw them at summer camp, singing "Pharaoh, Pharaoh" at the top of their lungs. I saw them in altar-call processionals at youth retreats—faces full of tears, dedicating and rededicating their lives to Jesus. I saw them eagerly building wheelchair ramps and painting houses on mission trips, desperate to participate in something bigger than themselves. I saw them at See You at the Pole rallies as they prayed in front of their schools for revival. Car washes. Chubby bunny. Polaroid camera scavenger hunts. They spent more time at the church than their parents (by far).

Then they graduated from high school. At most churches, this meant that they no longer had generationally optimized content or activities. Their only option was to attend "regular" church. If they wanted to engage beyond Sunday morning, it was through ministries designed for (and populated by) older generations. They went from student bands to robed choirs (or middle-aged bands), song sheets on overhead projectors to hymnals, from—let's be honest—fun to boredom. Much like my own experience after camp, the buttoned-up, stoic posture of church failed to connect with them.

So they left.

How would a millennial describe a sanctuary? I think they might say: *Why do you need a sanctuary?* Their sanctuary was sitting on a carpeted floor in a living room or church basement, or outside at a retreat. They wore pajama bottoms. They had their shoes off. They ate pizza and sang Jesus songs. They told stories about what was happening in their lives. And the church sanctuaries of "builders," boomers, and Gen Xers became irrelevant.

Last, we arrive at the three youngest generations: Gen Z (1997–2012), Gen Alpha (2013–24), and Gen Beta (2025–39). Since large-scale data on the religious habits of Gen Alpha and Gen Beta doesn't yet exist, we'll treat them as part of Gen Z for now.

These are the digital natives. They don't remember the world before smartphones, iPads, and on-demand digital content. It's a part of who they are. It's their portal to access entertainment, social connection, and basic information. If they read the Bible, it's probably on the YouVersion Bible app. If they watch Christian content, it's probably on TikTok. Like the millennials before them, the sanctuaries of builder and boomer generations may feel unfamiliar or even unnecessary in the wake of digital alternatives (notwithstanding some of the recent reports of Gen Z males, particularly in Great Britian, who are gravitating toward more traditional church spaces). (But, we'll talk more about emerging generations in Chapter Six.)

Moving Past "One Size Fits All"

Hopefully, what's abundantly clear after this exercise (and this chapter) is that a one-size-fits-all approach to church is not going to work. There's an old marketing adage: If you're trying to reach everyone, you're really reaching no one. I know the church isn't a marketing firm or a business. But people are still people. The decision to buy a product, participate in a cause, or affiliate with a religious organization is, in the end, driven by human desires, pain points, and dreams. If you can speak their language, if you can do a good job at translating, you can reach them. You can show them a new life in Jesus.

Who are you trying to reach? As Darrell Hall points out in *Speaking across Generations*, "The generation that preachers address directly by speaking about their needs, appreciating their formative experiences, and using language they prefer will be present in their congregations."[17]

The rest of this translation process will work for any generation you choose. If your church is in the middle of retirement communities, this process will work to reach them. Your church may be in a neighborhood that has completely changed culturally since the church was planted or built. This process will help you reach them. However, for the remainder of this book, we will assume you are trying to reach younger generations. For our purposes, this means young families (Gen X and millennial parents with Gen Z, Gen Alpha, and Gen Beta children).

What about singles? What about widows and empty-nesters and other ages and stages: Aren't we trying to reach them? Of course we are. And that's precisely the point of the process I'm giving you in this book. The idea is that you can take this 4D Process and apply it to *anyone you're trying to reach*. However, since there are so many possible targets, we're going to focus on the demographic I believe represents the most urgency for our churches (and the one many churches struggle to reach): young families (or, more specifically, families with young children). And, as we go, I'll share with you what my church did to start reaching them so you can see some real examples of possible gospel translating—not so you can copy them, but so they can inspire you to do what *you* need for *your* context.

Now that we know who we are and who we're trying to reach (young families for now), your SVT is ready to start the gospel translation process. Kotter's second step in leading change is to, after developing urgency, establish a guiding coalition.[18] The SVT is the coalition that will act as the vision steering team. The next step will be to enter the Discern stage. This is where you'll learn their language(s) to bring the gospel to bear in their lives. By understanding their culture, you will begin to discern what ministry initiatives you can launch to reach them.

For Further Thought: Generational Sifting

- When was the last time your church had a lot of young families? Why were they coming? What were you doing the same/different than you're doing now? What new opportunities could you create?
- In what ways has your congregation tried to reach young families in the last five years? What seems to be the biggest challenge to reaching them? What would need to be true to reach them?
- Without doing any research, try to brainstorm a list of things you know about young families. You'll test this list later when you begin your research.

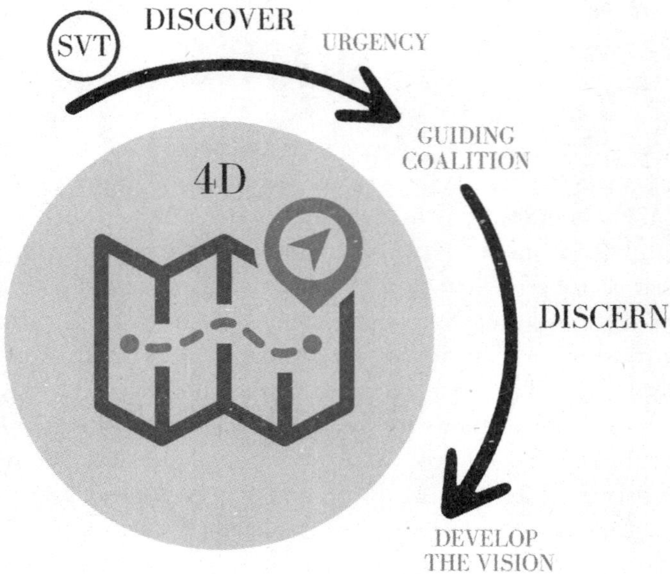

Figure 3.1. Generational Chart

Generational Quick View

Builders (born 1928–45)	Traditional Sanctuary	Post-WWII, God and country, church is "American way of life"
Boomers (born 1946–64)	Contemporary Sanctuary	"Generation gap" children of the 1960s, Jesus music and birth of contemporary worship
Gen X (born 1965–80)	Intimate Sanctuary	MTV generation, latchkey kids, huge media influence, desire for authenticity
"Millennials" Gen Y (born 1981–96)	No Sanctuary	Internet generation, world got smaller, cafeteria-tray approach to life
Gen Z (born 1997–2012)	Hybrid Sanctuary	Digital natives, grew up in the pandemic, smartphones are a way of life
Gen Alpha (born 2013–24) Gen Beta (born 2025–39)		

Chapter Four

THE ART OF TRANSLATION

I have become all things to all people so that by all possible means I might save some.
—1 CORINTHIANS 9:22

Learn avidly. Question repeatedly what you have learned. Analyze it carefully.
Then put what you have learned into practice intelligently.
—EDWARD COCKER

One of the traps I've discovered in ministry is that, if I'm not careful, I can talk about God more than I talk to God. It takes constant vigilance to fight this. If I don't make intentional time to be with God, it creates unintentional distance. Of course, this is true in any relationship—marriage, friendship, etc. If you're never together, it's hard to stay connected.

It's like my friends from high school. I joined a Facebook Group a few years back, where many post pictures of their kids, vacations, and glamour shots of their food (the real purpose of social media). Recently, I had a chance to reconnect with some of them at a football stadium dedication in honor of our late head coach. For the most part, it had been thirty-two years since I'd seen any of them in person. Let's just say, a lot of life happened in that time.

It was great to reminisce and laugh and catch up. However, what I realized is that, despite knowing what many of them ate for dinner on vacation, I don't really *know* them anymore. I know *about* them, and yes, I used to know them. But so much time has passed between us that we're not familiar enough to be the friends we used to be. We could be close again, but not without spending time together.

So what? What does this have to do with translating the gospel for young families? Well, let's say that one of those old friends is looking for a church. After discovering that I'm a pastor, they ask me: *Jason, do you know any good churches in X town?* (I do get this question a lot—just not from old high school friends.) Now, I could do a Google search. I could navigate a few websites and watch online services to get a feel. I could even email a pastor and ask some questions. The problem is, because I don't really know my old friend anymore, I have no clue what would be a good fit. I don't know why they're looking (maybe something happened at the last church). I don't know their baggage. What if they love traditional worship and I send them to a contemporary church? Or what if it's the opposite? I don't know if they have kids or, if they do, what kind of ministry opportunities they want for them. They may be young empty nesters. The point is, I don't know what I don't know. That makes it really challenging to know how to reach them.

Who are the young families you're trying to reach? Maybe you can think of a handful of specific names and faces. Or maybe you just know them from a distance. As you drive by your local park on the weekend, you see them swarming the soccer fields and carrying their coolers, strollers, and camp chairs. They're behind you at the grocery store checkout, making a commotion as exasperated parents defend the strategically placed candy (not even the iPad can seem to distract the kids). They trick or treat in your neighborhood. They come to town tree lightings. They're your neighbors. But do you really *know* who they are? Or do you just know *about* them? It's only when you know them that you'll be able to reach them.

Stage Two: Discern

The Discern stage is about placing your finger on the pulse of who you're trying to reach so you can develop effective strategies to reach them—your strategic vision. By reaching them, I mean helping them take a step (wherever they are in their journey) toward Jesus. In the translation process, it's figuring out how to land the never-changing truth of Jesus Christ into the ever-changing language of culture. How do we learn the languages of our young families? It begins with listening.

How do we truly understand anyone? How do we know their needs, hopes, dreams, or fears? By listening to them (I know, crazy). But you'd be surprised at how little listening is happening in churches. Most churches don't listen at all, primarily because they think they already know what young families need.

It's like my kids getting ready for school—a daily exercise in listening futility. My wife and I say things to them like, *Hey, don't forget your water bottle*, or, *Did you pack your lunch?* And what do we get for our wonderfully helpful reminders? Typically, one of two responses. The first is annoyance. After all, they don't need reminding because they already know (duh, Dad)—this often comes with a free eye roll. Or second, they weren't listening at all (even though they were looking right at us) and say, *huh?*

I believe the biggest reason churches can't seem to connect with young families is because they simply aren't listening to them. Thankfully, this problem is fixable. The Discern stage is the listening stage, or more accurately, the active listening stage. Active listening is responsive. It's head nods and verbal cues that show you're listening. It's "when you not only hear what someone is saying, but also attune to their thoughts and feelings. It turns a conversation into an active, non-competitive, two-way interaction."[1] It's this kind of listening that was baked into Jesus's own ministry strategy (for example, the Samaritan woman at the well and the disciples on the road to Emmaus). It should be part of our strategy as well.

Listening in Two Directions

Active listening, when it comes to reaching across generations with the gospel, isn't merely sociological—it's also supernatural. Discernment, after all, is an activity of the Holy Spirit within us. We can't just best-practice our way to faithful translation; we have to listen our way to it. As Romans 12:2 urges, we must not "conform to the pattern of this world, but be transformed by the renewing of [our] mind[s]. Then [we] will be able to test and approve what God's will is." In other words, if we attune ourselves to the movement of the Spirit, we'll know what God wants us to do.

God will speak. God will show up. God will lead you where you're supposed to go. But you must invite God into this process. One of the key purposes of the Discern stage (and the entire 4D Process) is to intentionally help your team (and congregation) draw near to God. Study Scripture together at the beginning of your meetings. Pray for the young families you're trying to reach. Actively listen as you ask God to reveal the right strategies and insights.

The translation process, if done correctly, will lead to spiritual growth. This is one of the unheralded byproducts of revitalization, yet it may be the most critical. Why? Because, suppose everything you do to reach young families doesn't, for some reason, work at all (highly unlikely, but let's assume it's true). Does it mean you failed? Nope. By engaging in the process, risking comfort for the sake of reach, and drawing nearer to God, you succeeded, even if not a single new family walks through the door. Why? Because you helped a congregation awaken to God's presence and grow in faithfulness. The worst thing that can happen is that you have a more spiritually alive church on your hands. Would you take it? Me too.

Becoming Resident Aliens

When Wycliffe Bible Translators sets out to translate the Bible into another language, they don't start translating until they understand the culture. Sometimes, this takes years. Why? Because translation is incarnational. It's making the Word "flesh" for a particular time, place, and people. This takes time. It takes relationships. It takes living in it to really get it. I can read all about the history of Greece. I can learn the language and study their customs, geography, and traditions. But it's nothing compared to becoming a resident.

I believe this is what Paul was getting at when he said, "I have become all things to all people so that by all possible means I might save some" (1 Cor. 9:22). We must become residents in the culture we hope to reach. We don't need to become like them, but we do need to truly understand how they think and feel. Otherwise, we run the risk of mistranslating.

Let's say you're a grandparent. How do you connect with your grandkids? Maybe you don't have a TikTok account (good, you'll live longer). Maybe you have no idea what your grandkids are saying when they come to your house and say things like, "Grandpa, that's lit," "Grandma, that's cap," or "These mashed potatoes are gas." But the good news is that you have a relationship with them. Over time, you can start to understand. You can learn their language and perceive their needs. You can meet them where they are because you love them as they are. This should be the posture of our churches: we meet people where they are because we (and God) love them as they are.

This doesn't necessarily mean God wants them to *stay* where they are, and that's where translation comes in. Translation is an act of love, seeking to build bridges of understanding between us and those we're trying to reach. As the Wycliffe website explains:

> This means the Bible translator's role is complex: 1) to determine what the source text says; 2) to analyze what the source text means; 3) and then to discover how best to express that meaning in the intended language. In order to do this well, Bible translators need to discover how best to communicate God's message using cultural, linguistic and theological bridges.[2]

This is how we do the mission. It's how we fulfill the Great Commission, the *Missio Dei* (mission of God). We must reside in culture (both sociological and generational) even if we aren't of that culture. We become resident aliens, doing life together with young families to love them. It's precisely in the loving that we start understanding how best to express the gospel in the intended language.

This loving is mission critical. You'll never reach a culture you don't love. Why? Because you won't be willing to sacrifice or face the discomfort it takes to build bridges, seek understanding, or change preferred traditions to reach them. You'll never meet them where they are because you don't love them as they are. But once your hearts and minds are set on loving and listening, how do you learn their cultural language? What are the mechanics?

Learning Is Both an Art and a Science

As any first-year biblical Greek student will tell you, translation is not always a straightforward endeavor. It is as much an art as it is a science. It's not only about word-for-word accuracy but an interpretive dialogue between the words on the page and the "tone, mood, attitude, feeling, [and] voice of a speaker."[3]

Learning a cultural language is not unlike learning a spoken language—there is a methodology. Before you can speak it, you need to hear it. As you hear it, you start to learn a new alphabet and the rules of grammar. Then, you start practicing these new sounds on your own lips. In a similar way, your team should talk to young families and get to know how they process the world around them (see the questions at the end of this chapter). If you don't have any young families in your church already, see if you can rent them (just kidding).

But let's say that's the case: That there are no young families in your church. What do you do? You'll need to get creative. First (I recommend doing this even if you do have young families around), you should find some books or resources to help familiarize yourself with their language(s). Read and discuss them. Learn the alphabet. Learn how they feel about Jesus, Christians, sports, vacations, education, entertainment—everything you can. (There's a list of resources at the end of the chapter.)

Discernment happens through listening, and listening can be both direct and indirect. You'll eventually need to talk to the people you're trying to reach; however, you can learn a lot about them through other sources along the way. It's like painting by numbers. You can connect a lot of dots formed by the information. This outlines the picture. Then, you color in the picture by having conversations with young families. Once the picture is complete, you'll be able to discern how to reach them.

Connecting the Dots

There's a study that came out of Stanford University that became a book: *Dreams of the Overworked.* It uncovers the pressures on young families of "living, working, and parenting in the digital age."[4] The authors, Christine Beckman and Melissa Mazmanian, studied "nine families with school-age children living in Southern California between 2012 and 2015."[5] What they discovered was that there were three cultural myths that were causing a tremendous amount of stress on parents of young children: the need to be an ideal worker, to be perfect parents, and to have a great body.

The first myth that these parents feel is the myth of the ideal worker. The ideal worker is reflected in the old saying: *When they say jump, I ask, How high?* It's always being available to the workplace and giving it your best attention, energy, and devotion. It's always saying yes to late hours, overtime, and being the consummate team player.

The perfect parent myth "is about dedicating one's entire self to the project of childrearing."[6] It's about treating all available time as quality time with your children. This includes but is not limited to: coaching youth sports, taking trips and special vacations, and being present whenever the occasion calls for it. Of course, we can see the tension immediately: you can't be the ideal worker and the perfect parent.

Last, the myth of having the ultimate body goes beyond leading a healthy lifestyle. There is pressure for these parents to "do more to cultivate their bodies."[7] It's about living up to the expectation of physical beauty and perfection. This, of course, you can't do if you're busy jumping high for your job or for your children. This is what's causing so much stress. "It is fundamentally impossible to achieve even one of these myths, no less all three."[8]

Dreams of the Overworked is an example of how to start connecting the dots with the parents you're trying to reach. The three myths, for example, can inform your conversations with them. It's like pre-interview research on a talk show. The research helps determine the right questions to ask. You'll validate and color in the rest through face-to-face dialogue.

What's the takeaway? That if we can begin to understand the pain points, we start learning their language. If we can learn the language, we have a better shot at landing the gospel of Jesus Christ in their lives. While books and articles are incredibly helpful, it's important not to skip the next step: find a way to talk to them.

Coloring in the Picture

Again, you may not have young families in your building. But I bet you have parents, grandparents, and maybe even great-grandparents in your sanctuary. Invite them to become "journalists." Hand them a few key questions to ask their kids and grandkids and report back to the team. For those young families who don't go to church, maybe start with: *Why don't you currently attend a church?* There is nothing like just asking directly. Then, try to understand them: *What are the top three concerns you have for your family?* Or, *What are you most excited about regarding your family?* Then ask: *If you did go to church, what would you be looking for?* And, *What would keep you there?* Or, if they do go to church, *What about that church attracted you? Why do you still go there? How is it helping you in your life?*

Maybe you're worried that this process (like a spoken language) will take too much time. Yes, it will take time. But as my grandpa always said, you measure twice so you only have to cut once. By taking the time to learn about young families in your community, you will save time, money, and energy. It will insulate you from the desperate impulse to just do something to reach them, not really knowing if that something is what they want or need. You find that out by doing some sifting.

Cultural Sifting

Tim Keller, in his book *Center Church*, discusses the importance of what he calls cultural sifting. This is the process of applying the gospel to a particular culture and determining how it both affirms and challenges that culture to redeem it. Take Paul, for example, and his ministry moment in Athens (as recorded in Acts 17).

Paul was invited to participate in a philosophical discussion, held atop the Areopagus, "or Mars Hill, one of the more prominent topological features of ancient Athens."[9] At this meeting, he leveraged the particularities of Athenian cultural language (specifically, their philosophical and religious traditions) to translate the gospel:

> Paul then stood up in the meeting of the Areopagus and said: "People of Athens! I see that in every way you are very religious. For as I walked around and looked carefully at your objects of worship, I even found an altar with this inscription: to an unknown god. So you are ignorant of the very thing you worship—and this is what I am going to proclaim to you." (Acts 17:22–23)

He first affirmed the culture, and then he challenged the culture so he could say something true about God. It's this sifting process that leverages culture to proclaim Jesus.

Learning how to read biblical Greek and Hebrew is pretty intense (right, pastors?). I remember how much work it took. I remember late nights reviewing flashcards, class notes, and homework assignments. In the end, I didn't become a fluent speaker (or even reader) of these languages. But I learned enough to properly use the tools to fill in the gap. In your translation process with young families, you just need to know enough to use the tools. It's time to put the cultural translator in use: theological visioning.

Developing a Theological Vision

The next step is to begin the translation. It's time to start connecting the timeless truth of the gospel into the particularity of their everyday lives. This is the third step in Kotter's process: "develop a vision and a strategy."[10] The method we will use to frame this activity is Tim Keller's model of developing a theological vision: "a vision for what you are going to do with your doctrine in a particular time and place."[11]

In *Center Church*, Keller describes this process like computer programming: "If you think of your doctrinal foundations as 'hardware' and of ministry programs as 'software,' it is important to understand the existence of something called 'middleware.'"[12] Middleware is the translative computer language that connects hardware and software. A theological vision is like middleware. It's the interpretive movement that "leads church leaders to make good decisions on how to worship, disciple, evangelize, serve, and engage culture in their field of ministry."[13] This is the heavy lifting of the translation process.

For example, in 2013, our SVT at Tower Hill Church saw a need to help young fathers grow deeper in discipleship. Our theology tells us that spiritual formation is the process of losing oneself to become more like Christ. This transformation is an activity of the Holy Spirit. One of the ways the Spirit works this transformation is through Bible study and prayer. That's our doctrinal commitment.

The problem was that the men we were trying to reach had two barriers: a lack of time (particularly for New York City commuters) and a mindset of Bible study as obligation and spiritual box-checking. They wanted a regular experience that helped them grow closer to Jesus, one that was more casual than a typical Bible study at church and more flexible with time. We started a Bible study in a leader's basement that met every other Wednesday at 8 p.m. The format was to hang out and catch up for about twenty minutes, play a video or read a passage, and then have time to pray for one another's needs. We were able to create a bridge between our theology and the culture we were trying to reach. That's developing a theological vision.

In a way, it's really about meeting needs. In late 2020 and early 2021, we had what seemed like a hundred baptism requests for babies born during the COVID-19 pandemic. I remember, with the gathering restrictions in place, all of the anxiety parents were feeling during that cultural moment. In May 2021, there was an article in our local paper, the *Asbury Park Press*, titled "Pandemic

Babies' Parents Have Fears." In it, Gabriela Miranda writes, "Some parents who have welcomed babies during the pandemic have expressed fear of exposing their newborns to COVID-19. This fear has taken center stage, and they are struggling with when and how to socialize their babies."[14]

After I read this article, I shared it with our leadership and asked: *How can we meet the need with a theological vision?* If the hardware is creating fellowship and spiritual friendships, and if the software is the need to socialize the babies (and moms), then what is the middleware? The answer was to set up some baby playdates (outside, due to the restrictions). Not only did we get to know these families better, but they bonded with one another. Today, there are many small groups, friend groups, and active and engaged members that all started with that simple act of meeting needs.

In *Dreams of the Overworked*, Beckman and Mazmanian call this scaffolding. It's asking: *How can we help young families live, work, and parent in the digital age? How can we build a support system around their lives?* Maybe they need playdates. Or childcare. Or a group of like-minded parents. Or carpools to travel baseball. How can we meet their needs (which is meeting and loving them where they are)? It's what Rev. Robert Schuller (of Crystal Cathedral fame) once said: "Find a need and meet it. Find a hurt and heal it. Find a problem and solve it."[15]

Where to Start the Gospel Translating

When it comes to young families, where do we begin to meet their needs? There are four key areas for churches to consider (in order): worship, next gen ministries (cradle to college), evangelism, and adult spiritual formation. The pace of the 4D Process will slow down here, as we take a closer look at each area in the next few chapters as part of the Discern stage. There are other areas to be sure, but for the scope of this book, we'll concentrate on these.

Before we begin, here's a word of encouragement—it's going to feel like you're going painfully slow. Embrace it. It means you're probably doing something right. It's like the 1990 Kevin Costner film *Dances with Wolves*. It's the story of Union Army lieutenant John Dunbar and his interaction with a Sioux tribe during the Civil War. When both Dunbar and the medicine man of the tribe, Kicking Bird, finally overcome their fears enough to talk to each other, the linguistic progress is painfully slow. Likewise, your cultural language learning will feel that way at first. But what we learn from Dunbar is that persistence works. By immersing himself in the culture (living with them), he becomes fluent quickly, which, in the end, saves the entire tribe.

We must make our residence with young families so we can know how to be for them. We need to do life with them so we can know what to say and how to say it. This is the art of translation, which takes time, focus, and love. Remember, if we don't love the culture we're trying to reach, we'll never reach them. That doesn't mean we agree with everything in that culture, but we seek to understand for the sake of saving the tribe.

I know this sounds hard. It is, but maybe not in the way you think. Think about it this way: Let's say you're Christmas shopping for your kids or grandkids, and they've given you a list of what they want. It's not all that hard to pick what you're going to buy, as you weigh cost versus impact versus *Am I really going to buy the eight-year-old a survival knife?* (True story: My grandma got my little brother a Rambo-style knife one Christmas.)

Once you decide on which gift to buy, it's just a matter of making the purchase. The hard part is the shopping or gift-selection process. That's the part that takes time and searching and evaluating. Similarly, the hard part won't be the ministry opportunities you'll offer (because your families will have given you their shopping list). The hard part is committing to the process. It will take discipline to keep your congregation focused enough to keep moving forward. It will take determination to push through discomfort. It will take courage to implement the changes.

For Further Thought: Generational Sifting

- Do you already have some Gen X, millennial, or Gen Z (or younger) church attenders? They will be your test market. Find a way to start engaging them in conversation about their hopes, dreams, hurts, and spiritual longings. Find out what their biggest need is, and then you'll be able to start thinking about how to fill it.
- Pick a generational resource below, and begin reading it with your SVT. Read a chapter, and then ask three questions. Continue as you work through the book together.
- After the first two steps, make a list of the current ministry programs you offer and whether or not they will connect with young families. Assess whether they can be adapted to work well or if there are better options you're currently not offering.

Generational Resources

- *Aliens among Us: Ten Surprising Truths about Gen Z* by Steven Robertson
- *Generations: The Real Differences between Gen Z, Millennials, Gen X, Boomers, and Silents—and What They Mean for America's Future* by Jean M. Twenge
- *Speaking across Generations: Messages That Satisfy Boomers, Xers, Millennials, Gen Z, and Beyond* by Darrell E. Hall
- *You Found Me: New Research on How Unchurched Nones, Millennials, and Irreligious Are Surprisingly Open to Christian Faith* by Rick Richardson
- *Next Sunday: An Honest Dialogue about the Future of the Church* by Nancy Beach and Samantha Beach Kiley

A Few Classic Resources

- *Growing Young: 6 Essential Strategies to Help Young People Discover and Love Your Church* by Kara Powell, Jake Mulder, and Brad Griffin
- *Generation Me: Why Today's Young Americans Are More Confident, Assertive, Entitled—And More Miserable Than Ever Before* by Jean M. Twenge
- *The Emerging Church: Vintage Christianity for Emerging Generations* by Dan Kimball
- *Marketing to Gen Z: The Rules for Reaching This Vast and Very Different Generation of Influencers* by Jeff Fromm and Angie Read

Chapter Five

CLOSING THE GAP IN WORSHIP

We worship God because God created us to worship Him. Worship is at the center of our existence, at the heart of our reason for being.
—HUGHES OLIPHANT OLD

The first of the four primary ways we can help young families connect with God is through worship. It's both the epicenter of God's transformative work in us and the most likely landing place for young families to show up at church. Of course, it goes beyond just a worship service. Romans 12:1–2 describes it as nonconformity to the patterns of this world and greater conformity to the patterns of Christ. As Richard Foster puts it: "To worship is to experience Reality, to touch Life. It is to know, to feel, to experience the resurrected Christ in the midst of the gathered community. . . . Worship is our response to the overtures of love from the heart of the Father."[1] It's a supernatural reality, as we touch life and connect with God.

Worship is always tethered to a sociological reality as well. It's about people gathering under one roof, where friendships are formed between strangers, seekers, and longtime Christ followers. It's where outsiders show up looking for God and discover a family that's looking with them. The worship service is where people feel seen and valued. It's where they feel inspired, challenged, and exhorted to follow Jesus more closely.

Worship isn't just about a particular form or style. It's about giving glory and honor to the king, which can happen in numerous forms and styles. That said, the way you lead worship matters. Let's put it this way: God is the one who feeds people, but our job is to set the table. It's a partnership. Our job is to set the table in such a way that people want to sit down and eat. Unfortunately, churches have struggled to do this well, and perhaps it's no surprise that much of the disconnect between generations "has a lot to do with most churches' worship services."[2]

A Bad Worship Service Becomes a Barrier

I heard a saying years ago: *It's a sin to bore people with the gospel.* While I don't agree that it's a sin, I do agree that it's a major problem for far too many churches. Let me start by saying, I don't believe there's such a thing as bad worship (as long as it's theologically sound). After all, where two or three are gathered in Jesus's name, he is with them. But I do believe there is such a thing as a bad worship service.

This is where you might think I'm going to beat up on traditional, "builder"-style worship. Worship quality, however has little to do with style. I've seen bad contemporary, bad traditional, bad Taizé, bad vespers—you get the idea. What do I mean by bad? I mean an experience so uncompelling, so ill-planned and executed, so generationally out-of-touch that it makes it less likely for a worshiper to connect with God. It makes them want to avoid the table altogether. If they do worship, it's in spite of, not because of, the service.

I know that sounds harsh, but bear with me here. A bad service will pull you out of worship, not draw you in. I'm sure you've been in a situation where a new preacher or an inexperienced singer or liturgist is so nervous they can barely hold it together. You find yourself feeling their nerves. As their lips tremble and hands shake, you start praying that they'll be able to get through it in one piece.

Do you think that experience drew people into worship? Maybe some of your older members are so good at compartmentalizing that stuff that it has little negative effect on their experience. But I doubt it. We human beings just aren't wired for focusing on more than one thing at a time. If you're focused on the shaky liturgist, it's hard to be focused on God. Let me be clear: God is already present when we gather in his name to worship. But we aren't always present for God. It's not that it has to be a show, with professional singers and state-of-the-art video walls, but it has to be competent enough to not be a distraction.

Competence, however, is a double-edged sword. If the praise singer launches into a vocal riff in the middle of every song, it will become a distraction. If the electric guitarist plays a blues solo in the middle of "Oceans," that will be a distraction. Anything that pulls you away from worshiping God with your whole heart is a competence problem.

But it's not just a lack of competence that makes for bad worship services. It's also a lack of cultural relevance. We have to be careful with the word *relevance*, which has been used to justify a multitude of sins. Just like Bill in the German bar, most young families won't feel at home with traditional styles of worship because it's not in their language.

Since the majority of mainline denominational worship services are in the language of "builders" and boomers, there is "an increasing abandonment of traditional churches by the disillusioned post-1945 generations."[3] The unavoidable truth is that young families overwhelmingly prefer more contemporary worship experiences. This is because that style has a closer generational proximity.

Could that change? Could there be a pendulum swing back? Could Gen Alpha and Gen Beta crave a simpler, more traditional practice of worship? Absolutely! But I haven't seen it yet. Waiting for younger generations to come back to what older generations prefer is how we got in this problem in the first place.

Is Changing Worship Worth the Work?

Of all the things you're ready and willing to change, worship may not be at the top of your list. It's not because you don't think it's important. It's because you'd rather change easier things—smaller, less threatening things. Maybe tweak Sunday school or youth group or outreach programs, but worship? *That's too big to change.* That's why most pastors try to avoid it. Or they try to make compromises and end up back where they started without any noticeable change. But worship isn't too big to change; it's too big to ignore. It's the engine for the overall health of your church and a key area to address when it comes to attracting young families.

Changing worship doesn't mean replacing your current worship service (I highly recommend you don't). You are either adding a completely new service (preferred) or adapting your current one to help speak to multiple generations. Your strategy will depend on the quality of your discernment. Ask: *How can we bring the gospel through worship for this particular demographic?*

For now, let's consider: How do you work toward a good worship service, one that is competent and relevant for the young families you're trying to reach? How do you encourage them to sit at the table and "taste and see that the Lord is good" (Ps. 34:8)? How do you start reimagining a worship service to draw them into a worship experience?

Tower Hill's Story—Translating Worship

Reaching young families through worship was the single most impactful change we made at Tower Hill. But when I started as senior pastor in 2012, I didn't think it would be as much work as it was. If I were a guest on a Sunday morning back then, I would've concluded that we had a healthy, vibrant church: beautiful campus, well-attended traditional worship, forty-member choir, youth bell (and vocal) choirs, and a regional reputation for high-quality, traditional music. If I would have taken a quick look at the church budget and endowment fund spreadsheets, I would have said: *This church is in good shape*. But looks can be deceiving.

While growing up in the Los Angeles. area, my family and I often went to Universal Studios. One of the attractions was a tram tour of the old movie sets (including the town center of Hill Valley from *Back to the Future*). On the tour, they revealed the secret to how they built these sets so quickly and cheaply. They only built the front façade. If you looked at it from behind, you would just see simple wood or metal framing—an empty shell.

Tower Hill was a bit of a movie set. While the façade showed health, it had been in internal decline for decades. The church peaked in membership in around 1973, with 2,954 members. Forty years later, in 2013, that was down to 885 (with an average of about three hundred in weekly worship). Not exactly a megachurch, but certainly still large by US denominational standards. This is precisely what made it such a challenge. The congregation was unhealthy but not unhealthy enough for people to feel the urgency. The church was still operating as if nothing had changed. In many ways, people were acting like they were still part of a 2,954-member church. This mindset created a host of resource problems.

It's kind of like having prediabetes. You're not sick enough to need medication, but if you ignore it, you'll not only develop diabetes, but it may be too late to reverse it. The remedy is to drastically alter your lifestyle before it's too late. While Tower Hill may not have been quite ready for that level of change, they at least noticed the signs of disease—primarily that they were hemorrhaging young families.

The good news was that the young families who were leaving told them why (which doesn't always happen). They wanted a contemporary worship service with Sunday school on Sunday morning. In 2007, the former pastor tried to scratch the contemporary itch by starting a Saturday night service. But it never really took off. The reason? It was more than just an itch.

On the one hand, families didn't want an ad hoc accommodation or a style with older generational preferences. They wanted an established Sunday morning worship experience in their own cultural language. When they didn't get it, many of them left for other churches.

In an attempt to stop the bleeding (and listen to what young families were saying), in 2011 (the year before I arrived), Pastor Theresa Swenson (acting as interim) pushed the elder board to move the Saturday night contemporary service to Sunday morning. The new worship service, in the fellowship hall, would run concurrently and share the Sunday school hour with the traditional worshipers. Did it work? Well, kind of.

The Saturday service averaged thirty-five to forty people per week. Once it was moved to Sunday morning, it instantly doubled to about seventy to seventy-five people in attendance. But attendance remained flat for about ten months after the initial bump. This is because the service itself was still not quite in the language of the culture Tower Hill was trying to reach: young families (Gen Xers at the time).

The cultural worship preferences of older generations were showing up (intentionally and unintentionally) in the new service. Why wouldn't they? After all, the praise band consisted almost entirely of boomers. The greeters were boomers. The service designers were boomers. The service primarily appealed to, you guessed it, boomers. This is what Bob Whitesel and Kent Hunter refer to as "cultural overhang."[4]

Eventually, this overhang (if left unchecked) can prevent the culture you're trying to reach from truly expressing worship in their *own* language. At first at Tower Hill, the service had a healthy contingency of young families, but by the end of that first year (by the time I showed up), guess which generation was most represented? Boomers. There were some Gen Xers, but they had all migrated from the traditional service. In other words, we weren't reaching new young families, just the families already in the room. What about millennials? We had a total of two. It was clear that more cultural translating was needed.

This is why I was hired. The church took a chance on me, its second-youngest (by one year) senior pastor since 1852, for two main reasons: one, because my family was in the young family demographic they felt that would be attractive to other young families; and two, because I had experience designing, launching, and growing contemporary services in traditional churches.

The initiative to move contemporary worship to Sunday morning saved a great deal of time. Typically, one of the early battles is simply convincing people that a new service is needed. The next is deciding when and where it will take place. But these questions were already answered and established by the time I came on board. This allowed me to focus squarely on digging deeper into the needs of young families and translating those needs into worship design (music, audiovisual support, and service elements/flow).

Did this work? Beyond my wildest expectations. Last Sunday (as I write this chapter), we had about 730 adults join us across two contemporary worship services. We also had another 275 in traditional worship. In all, there are about three thousand people that call Tower Hill church home, with hundreds of Gen Xers and millennials (young families). We're reaching more people now that at any other time in our history. Our heyday wasn't fifty years ago. It's today.

This isn't an overnight success story—it's the story of the 4D Process over twelve years. It's gospel translation. The exciting thing is that it's a repeatable process. You can do the same thing; it's not rocket science. We listened to young families, learned their generational language, and asked: *How can we optimize the worship service to meet their needs and present the gospel in a compelling way? How can we set the table well?* Or, to use our translation language, we developed and implemented our theological vision.

Maybe you're tempted to think: *Yeah, of course it worked; you already had three hundred people!* Okay, then let me tell you about my friend Randy. Randy is in his early seventies. About eight years ago, he started pastoring a church of five people in the Poconos in Pennsylvania. Today, his church is in a new building, and it regularly has seventy-five people attending worship (sometimes even a hundred). How did he do it? In part by optimizing worship for younger generations.

Active Listening

Let the meeting of needs inform the worship design. You can make decisions about music styles, multimedia tools, sound systems, and confidence monitors, etc. But you don't want to do that until you start asking families what they want. When they respond, listen. This is the step that often get skipped. *Well, young families want a rock band with lights, fog, and a soul-vibrating bass drum*. But what do *your* young families want? Maybe they want an acoustic café. Or maybe a jazz service or a Gregorian chanting service. The point is, you need to invite, listen, and respond.

At Tower Hill, we already knew they wanted a contemporary service. But by engaging them on the front end, we gleaned some valuable insights. This helped shape our theological vision: we started to see the needs so we could determine what to do. Below is a quick look at the needs we identified when redesigning our worship. Hopefully, they can help provide a few examples of what to look for.

Address the Time Crunch

Most parents who work in New York City but live in the suburbs wake up before the kids to catch the bus, train, or ferry to Manhattan. If there's any delay (which happens often), they may not get home until after their children have gone to bed. That means that some weeks, they don't get to see their kids very much. They're forced to fight an unrelenting, everyday inevitability: a deficit of time. This shaped our worship service design in a few ways.

First, it was a factor in determining when the service would start. We asked: *Is the service at the right time for these families?* Initially, the contemporary service started at 9:15 a.m. Even though young children tend to get up early, we kept hearing a desire for a later start. So we listened. After doing some research, we discovered that 10:30 a.m. was the most popular worship time for young families in the United States. So we moved the service to 10:30 a.m.

Second, it shaped our Sunday school model. We discovered that young families would rarely give us more than one hour on Sunday mornings. So we utilized a one-hour model where kids were invited to Sunday school during the service (after the first song). Instead of back-to-back worship and Sunday school, it was combined to utilize the same hour.

And third, it helped us shape the elements of the service. We started asking, *What is the stress of the time crunch doing to their souls? How could we intentionally leverage that pain point to help connect them with Jesus?* So we added a prayer time that feels like a mini retreat. Almost every Sunday, we'll invite them to take ninety seconds and connect with God as they need. We say something like: *If you're new here, this is a time we like to give back to you. It's a time to pray, sit, and listen as you need to. In this busy life, we don't often have quiet, so here is a time for you to be with God.* We then dim the lights so the room is dark, with the band playing quietly. At the end, the worship leader closes with a brief prayer. This hit a powerful chord for young families (and everyone in the room). Almost every week, there are people in tears by the time we finish.

Create the Right Environment

Environments are everything. For example, if I were choosing an environment for a deep, intimate conversation, I wouldn't pick a doctor's waiting room. (The fluorescent lights alone would kill the vibe.) Instead, I might choose a campfire. The warmth and glow of the embers are magical. The right environment can open you up to God, and the wrong one can close you up. Based on what we were hearing from our young families, there was a desire for a more casual, comfortable environment that was not only kid friendly, but kid preferred.

It's one thing to have a nursery. It's quite another thing to quickly usher a family into it the second their baby starts crying. Young parents told us that they often didn't feel welcome unless their kids were perfectly quiet. "Where are we supposed to take them if they cry?" one mom asked. "I mean, there's not a single space that feels like it was made for the kids to be in."

So we started improving our environments (physically and emotionally), training our people on how to navigate the inevitable noise kids make (and what a blessing that is). We made sure all the kids' spaces were clean. If the nursery looks like it hasn't been painted in forty years and the toys haven't been washed since the Reagan administration, no one wants to leave their baby in there.

When we were thinking through the worship experience, we realized how important it was to pay attention to what guests see.

When they show up, does it look like we're ready to host them? We'd never dream of inviting a first-time guest to a messy house for dinner. Likewise, we needed to make sure we were prepared to host. *Do guests know where to go? Is the campus clean and inviting? Does it look like we care that they're here? Does it feel like a campfire or a waiting room?*

Then, in worship itself, how are we helping these young families (many of whom have considerable baggage about church) feel comfortable enough to open themselves to God's voice through the service? How are we cultivating a comfortable spiritual environment? In many ways, we had to start thinking like a church plant: *How do we make them comfortable in worship? What are the obstacles that are preventing them from feeling at home?* Yes, the Holy Spirit will disrupt, confront, and convict in worship, which is decidedly uncomfortable. But how do we help them open up in the first place? Through the environment we create.

One of the obstacles was simply communication. We wanted to make sure our guests didn't feel like outsiders by using overly churchy or insider language. I remember, in my youth ministry days, I kept wondering what a narthex was. It was mentioned in announcements, meetings, and so on, but I felt too embarrassed to ask. Finally, I cornered my pastor and said, "I know I should know this, but can you tell me what a narthex is?" He laughed and said, "It's the lobby." Then why don't we just say "lobby"? With people who already feel like outsiders, why would we reinforce that feeling by using unnecessarily esoteric language?

The other critical aspect of communication, we discovered, was to give guests permission to be wherever they are in their faith journey. At several points in the service, we added language like: "If you're new here, this is how we take communion," or "You may not know what you believe about Jesus, but we're glad you're here—bring your questions!" Or (and I say this often), "It's okay to be exactly where you are in your faith journey, but I think God doesn't want to leave you there." This simple communication focus creates an emotional and spiritual welcome mat. It works hand in hand with the environment we're trying to create.

By listening and learning, we tried to set the table in the most appealing way possible. Loud music encourages shy people to sing. Slightly darkened rooms help people to be vulnerable. Many people are nervous when they first come. We do everything we can to ease those nerves. For example, we want someone who is a first-timer (maybe their first time ever to church) to feel comfortable. So, the band will often play a secular song as part of the pre-service music—like "Never Tear Us Apart" by INXS or "I Won't Back Down" by Tom Petty. What we hear from new families is that it completely disarms them and gives them a feeling that this church experience might be fun. If they're at ease emotionally, they'll open up spiritually.

Create Moments That Lead to Movement

At this point, you may be thinking: Oh, he's just talking about an attractional church or seeker-sensitive church model like Willow Creek, North Point, Life.Church, and others. Not exactly. Tower Hill is a Presbyterian church. We're pretty buttoned-up in our Reformed theology and fanatical about our polity. We believe worship moves from invocation to confession to proclaiming and responding to the Word. But we try to do it through the language of the people we're trying to reach.

Gen Xers and millennials are looking for inspiration. I believe it was Bono of U2 fame (although I can't find the quote) who once talked about how the band put together a live show. He said something like: *Everyone craves a moment of transcendence, so we try and give it to them.* Of course, a worship service is not a show. It's not just entertainment. It's helping people connect with the living God. But the principle holds true because this is how people (especially younger generations) are wired—they're looking for moments that lead to movement. Again, it's setting the table for God to feed them.

Most worship services (at least in mainline denominational churches) are pretty emotionally stagnant. Sometimes—during a political debate, for example—a news agency will show a real-time graphic of how independent voters respond to the candidates' answers. It looks kind of like a seismometer reading, fluctuating up and down. If we had a worship service version of this that measured engagement, I think it would look more like a straight line.

Moments are created through energy dynamics. A fast song sets up a warm welcome. A slow song sets up a deeper message. An energy change leads to emotional alertness. If the energy level is static, it lulls people to sleep. A worship service should look more like a sine curve than a straight line (see Figure 5.1). The particular combination of worship elements generates emotional and spiritual moments for the congregation. We're not interested in emotional manipulation (convincing someone, in an underhanded or self-serving manner, to do something they don't want to do), but we do want to use our human emotional dynamics to make sure they are awake to God.

Make Sure the Preaching Connects

Last but not least, our young families shared their desire for engaging messages. When I was fresh out of seminary, I preached like, well, a seminarian. It was all about academic rigor and the turning of a theologically precise phrase. This, of course, isn't a bad thing. However, it takes extra work to make sure it's engaging. A sermon isn't an exegesis paper. What I learned the hard way is that great theology does not guarantee a great (or even effective) sermon. Again, there's a supernatural and a sociological aspect to preaching.

God tells us (and we should believe it) that God's Word does not return empty "but will accomplish what I desire and achieve the purpose for which I sent it" (Isa. 55:11). Yet, a young man named Eutychus fell out a window and died because Paul's preaching was so boring (Acts 20:9). There's a tension there (clearly). Our job is to make sure our beautifully constructed theology isn't like listening to a white noise machine that puts people to sleep.

Sermons are usually optimized for auditory learning. But of the four learning styles (visual, auditory, reading/writing, and kinesthetic), 65 percent of people are visual learners.[5] Even if 35 percent are not, I'm willing to bet that all Gen Xers and millennials are visual engagers (because of the technology through which they experience the world around them). In other words, even if they're not primarily visual learners, they are more effectively engaged visually than in any other way. Thus, I adjusted my preaching style to be dialed in to the eyes as well as the ears—using robust sermon visuals to engage.

We learned pretty quickly that younger generations have less biblical knowledge, or even biblical familiarity, than older generations. I knew I couldn't assume such knowledge but had to start unpacking it step-by-step: biblical stories, connections, or theological terms all needed some level of explaining. While this can admittedly be tiring, it is mission critical to reach Gen Xers and millennials.

These weren't the only changes we made, but they were the main categories based on what we learned. Over the last twelve years, we've adjusted and tweaked these elements along the way. But this is what it looks like. This is how you effectively translate: you listen, get to know them, and figure out how best to land the gospel in their everyday lives.

Some church members have accused us of "dumbing down" worship with language changes like "lobby" instead of "narthex" or the absence of formal liturgy (a common assertion from traditional gatekeepers). (If "narthex" is a dealbreaker, you should probably put this book down.) Whenever this happened, I would always point them to Acts 15.

The Acts 15 Approach

If you recall, in Acts 15, the Council of Jerusalem was wrestling with what to do about the Gentiles joining the early church. There was some disagreement over whether or not they had to, essentially, become Jewish first. Andy Stanley, in his book *Deep and Wide*, reminds us that what was at stake was "circumcision along with not ten, but over six hundred commandments plus commentary."[6] After some deliberation, James stood up and told the Council: "It is my judgment, therefore, that we should not make it difficult for the Gentiles who are turning to God" (Acts

15:19). In other words: *If the cultural requirements are getting in the way or are preventing people from turning to God, we need to get rid of them.* So, the Council decided to boil all those six hundred commandments down to three.

Our takeaway from this is to constantly ask: *Are we making it more or less difficult for them to turn to God?* I suppose at the heart of the matter is a fundamental decision: Do you care more about the ninety-nine or the one? Do you care more about who you're trying to reach or who you're trying to keep? For me, it's an easy decision. Yes, I obviously care about both. But, if it's ever a choice between comfort for insiders or mission to outsiders, I'll pick mission every time. What about you? How will you start to calibrate your worship service for young families?

Tips: Launching a New Worship Service

- Know your why. When you know why you're doing something, it makes it easier and clearer as you make decisions. Knowing why you're launching/continuing contemporary worship will help the what and the how.
- Go on a field trip (or two). Why reinvent the wheel? Learn from churches that are doing it well (or even not so well). There are at least two different types of churches your task force should visit: churches like yours that do contemporary worship and churches that are larger and incredibly effective at contemporary worship.
- Focus on the environment. Make sure your worship environment is appealing: get rid of clutter, paint the walls, adjust the lighting—anything you can do to make it feel like home. Remember, the environment is also ambience, which can include pre-service music, coffee, etc.
- Don't blend styles (if you can help it). Most of the time, about 20 percent of the people love it, but 80 percent of the people you're trying to reach can't stand it.

- It's more than music. A contemporary worship service or an alternative to a traditional worship service should rethink all parts of the service. It's as much about feel and emotion as it is about song selection.
- Hire a worship leader. It rarely works to use your current traditional director because it's just a different kind of music.
- Upgrade audiovisual as much as you can afford. If you work with an audiovisual company, they should be able to help you with how to think of your system in stages and upgrades.
- Launch in a way that optimizes Sunday school. Saturday night services don't typically work well for Protestants unless you live in a college town and have an active college ministry. Offer worship service on Sunday morning, and Sunday school (for kids) is a must.

Figure 5.1. Dynamic Worship

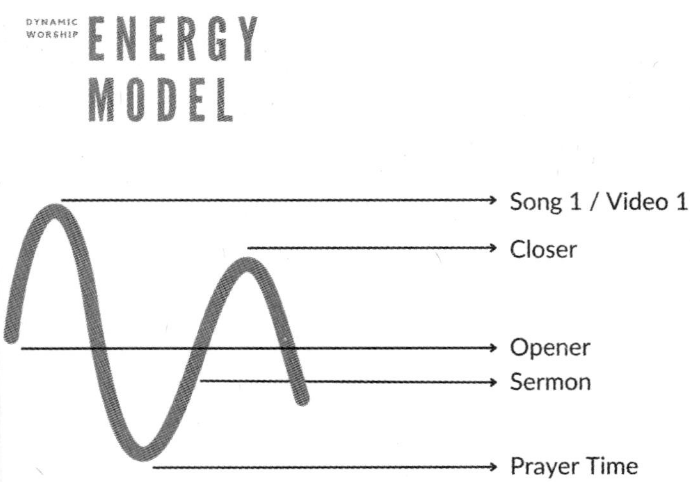

Chapter Six

CLOSING THE GAP WITH THE NEXT GEN

We ought to be ashamed of ourselves. . . . So many churches have no ministry to young people and that means they have no interest in the future.[1]

—LORD CAREY, FORMER ARCHBISHOP OF CANTERBURY

Another generation grew up who knew neither the Lord nor what he had done for Israel.

—JUDGES 2:10

On February 8, 2023, students at Asbury University gathered for their weekly Wednesday chapel service in Hughes Auditorium. Pastor Zach Meerkreebs, as part of his Love in Action series, invited students to let go of their hurt and experience God's perfect love.[2] He encouraged them to "stop striving and wearing such a heavy burden," and he said that "they cannot love until they've been loved by Jesus." At the end of his message, he prayed that students would be "filled with the love of God so they could pour out the love of God."

"Revive us by your Love," he prayed, as a piano played faintly. After the "amen," the student band began singing "Goodness of God":

> Your goodness is running after, it's running after me.
> Your goodness is running after, it's running after me.
> With my life laid down, I surrender now.
> I give You everything.
> Your goodness is running after, it's running after me.[3]

Students came forward. They prayed and worshiped together. And they didn't stop. They continued for hours. Then the next day. And the next. They continued for thirteen days after that, ending with "a service specifically for Gen Z students on February 23, 2023."[4] Talk of the event captured the attention of believers and nonbelievers alike. Students from other colleges, members of the media, and Christian celebrities spilled into the little town of Wilmore, Kentucky, over those two weeks, totaling "an estimated fifty thousand visitors." [5]

Many refer to the event as the Asbury Revival. The university has chosen a more nuanced approach in its description, calling it "a multiweek outpouring that some have described as a revival."[6] As Kevin Brown, the president of Asbury University, explained in *Cooperating with the Holy Spirit*: "In contrast to words like *revival, renewal,* or *awakening*—labels that carry nuanced theological significance—*outpouring* has enough space to harbor a variety of interpretations but is neutral enough to avoid defining something prematurely."[7]

Revival or outpouring? Either way, I'm sure Meerkreebs had no clue just how prophetic his prayer to revive would be. What's abundantly clear is this: God showed up. But, even more, the students also showed up for God.

Brown, in a *Christianity Today* article, said he saw something that gave him incredible hope during those sixteen days (whether officially considered a revival or not). "Gen Z is emerging as a corrective to the casual Christianity that has marked our religious landscape and characterized our de-churching movement . . . a sign of hope for the future of Christianity, its institutions, and the church."[8] In the middle of the dire news and bleak statistics, it's the next generation that seems hungry for God and humble enough to surrender.

But it's not just Gen Z college students. It's younger, Gen Alpha kids as well. There's a camp all three of my kids go to each summer: Spruce Lake in Canadensis, Pennsylvania. It reminds me of the camp I worked at in the 1990s. It's an old-school, kind of no-frills Christian camp, complete with cookouts, platform tents, arts and crafts, archery, zip lines, kayaking, swimming—and a laser-like focus on Jesus. It's my kids' happy place. It's the place that reinforced their faith in a powerful way.

Every year, I spend a week there as the camp pastor. Every week, they do their own version of a Hughes Auditorium altar call. It's not really an altar call—they simply invite the kids to talk with their counselor by lantern light. After a time of worship, the kids (only those who want to) make their way to an outdoor basketball court. There, each counselor is scattered about the cold cement, sitting beneath the stars, warming themselves by the lanterns in front of them. One by one, students are invited to sit by their counselor and talk. All those beautiful lights in the darkness. All those kids trying to sort out their life and faith—it's my favorite part of camp week.

As camp pastor, I usually have a spot with a lantern. I just have to make sure I bring a blanket or something to sit on, or I won't be able to get up again off that cement. Sometimes, I'll get a lot of traffic. As the pastor, I give a talk twice a day, so they know me. Naturally, faith topics related to the material come up. But not always. Sometimes, it's problems at home, problems at school, or some other type of problem. It's kind of rare that I get a kid who wants to put their faith in Jesus (most would already consider themselves Christians).

Last summer was different. I had a group of eleven-year-olds (maybe four or five) come to my lantern together. After they all sat across from me, one of them, a young girl, said, "We want to accept Jesus—how do we do that?" The other kids nodded their heads in agreement. So, I explained the gospel, and I led them in a prayer to receive Jesus as their Lord and Savior. Words can't express the joy I felt that night—and, I'm sure, heaven along with me (Luke 15:10).

Whenever this happens, something is awakened in me. I get this overwhelming sense that this is what I was put on this Earth to do. It's why I became a pastor in the first place. I think about the uphill climb it is for emerging generations to find Jesus, and I'm nearly moved to tears. That night, as we talked and prayed around that lantern on the cold, backache-inducing cement floor, I knew we were on holy ground. Just like the chapel floor of Hughes Auditorium.

What's Really Stopping Us?

A few years ago, I was invited to help an older (but still viable) church identify their key result areas (which we'll get to in Chapter Nine) so they could develop a plan to address them. One of their most obvious challenges was their lack of young families, which they hadn't had for fifteen years. Apparently, some kind of disagreement with the senior pastor led to a youth director's resignation. Most elders in the room said this was the tipping point. *Once the director left, the families dried up,* they said.

When I asked why they didn't replace the director, they said it was a financial decision (which is a common response). They assured me, however, that the youth ministry was now a priority, and they were dialed in on changing things. They had some newfound financing (a generous bequest) and were determined to hire another youth director to revitalize the ministry (and the church).

While I applauded their commitment to reaching younger generations, I asked, "What's the church going to do besides hire a new director? How are you calibrating your ministries toward the needs of young families?" They didn't know. But, they assured me, they were all-in on reaching the next generation. I asked them how much of their church budget was designated for this outreach. Nobody knew. After a few minutes of paper shuffling, someone pointed at a line item in the budget and said: *fifteen hundred dollars.*

Fifteen years of disconnect wouldn't be solved by fifteen hundred dollars. Nor would attempting to hire their way to relevance. These aren't bad things and may have been part of the solution. But they wouldn't have moved the needle on their own. They needed to rethink their entire approach. They needed to figure out how to optimize worship, Sunday school, evangelism, discipleship, and digital ministry for young families. They needed to first ask: *What kind of church do we need to become to reach the next generation?*

Most churches are unwilling to do this. To be clear, I'm not necessarily talking about trading handbells for fog machines or turning your sanctuary into a bounce house (as fun as that would be). I'm talking about the willingness to be uncomfortable for the sake of the gospel. I'm talking about trying to reach younger generations in the way we do church.

If we're not doing everything we can to reach the next generation, what are we doing? When we give account to God for our lives, what will our excuse be for not trying to reach the next generation? *I was afraid we'd have to change our music,* or *Sorry, we didn't have the money,* or *Our youth director left.* To not act is to act. It's to say, *God, the mission just isn't worth it, but my comfort is.*

Getting to Know the Next Gen

How do we help the next generation develop a life-changing personal relationship with Jesus? How do we help them see through the formidable anti-Christian obstacles they face in our culture—like Christian beliefs being portrayed in secular educational settings or social media as outdated or anti-intellectual? How do we position our churches in such a way that we attract and engage them with the gospel? We start by getting to know them.

Let's take a closer look at Gen Z (1997–2012). Then we'll discuss some possible strategies to reach and engage them. Again, as we mentioned in Chapter Three, since large-scale generational data on Gen Alpha is still limited (and Gen Beta was just born), we will focus on what we know about Gen Z. Due to generational proximity, there will certainly be some cultural overlap, and there will probably be more similarities than differences. In my own family, I have a Gen Z college student, a Gen Z high school student, and a Gen Alpha middle school student. The oldest and youngest are separated by six years. What I've observed, anecdotally, is that there isn't much daylight between the two regarding how they engage the world around them.

According to a research report from Barna, "How Teens around the World Relate to Jesus," "The profile that emerges from the aggregated data, [are] words like *optimistic, engaged, malleable, curious, authentic, inclusive,* and *collaborative*."[9] I'll highlight a few of these research-based characteristics, along with a couple others I've discovered firsthand. While this brief overview is not intended to be comprehensive, it can be a good starting point as you begin to consider strategies for effective gospel translation.

They're Spiritually Open

Gen Z is quickly earning a reputation as the spiritually open generation.[10] This is a surprising development based on overall church engagement numbers. It's downright shocking, considering that Gen Z is still the most likely generation to identify as atheists. But, what the research is also showing is that it's not because of an animosity toward Jesus (or the Christian faith) but an ignorance about him. They've just never heard the stories. Why? Because they're not in the building.

I often think of the disciple Thomas in John 20. The poor guy had one moment of doubt, and he's forever "doubting Thomas." But he didn't doubt because he wasn't open; he doubted because he was the only one not in the room when Jesus appeared (which I think is perfectly reasonable). I feel like this is the case with the next generation. They don't believe because they're not in the room. But they are absolutely open to seeing and touching his wounds for themselves. Like Kevin Brown, president of Asbury University, said, "There is a trenchant meaning vacuum in our country fostering a sweeping spiritual hunger"[11] in the next generation.

This is showing up in recent research. According to "How Teens around the World Relate to Jesus,"[12] teens and young adults (eighteen to twenty-five) are hungry to learn about Jesus (about 50 percent). More than half (58 percent) of Gen Z adults continue to identify as Christian (Catholic, Protestant, or other Christian traditions). Around half (despite low Scripture engagement) say their lives have been transformed by the message of the Bible. Even one in five non-Christian Gen Z adults are open to Scripture-based experiences and conversations. When you add experiences like a revival at Asbury University, Spruce Lake Camp, and scores of others, there is incredible hope for their future faith.

Here's the important question you'll need to wrestle with as a church team: *If the next generation is so spiritually open and hungry, why are we seeing them less and less at church? Why are there fewer young families with Gen Z teens and Gen Alpha grade-schoolers?* There's clearly a distance and a dissonance. But what, specifically, is causing it?

Jesus Isn't the Problem

A lot of people believe that Gen Z is disinterested in Christianity. Some will say it's because they're more liberal than older generations and that the Christian faith just doesn't fit in their worldview. Of course, they are more liberal, particularly around issues of human sexuality, mostly because that's the generational water they swim in. But out of the six living generations in our country, name one generation that wasn't more liberal than their parents on some issues.

Liberal or not, based on my own observations of my kids, their friends, and what the research tells us, their liberal worldview clearly isn't hindering their openness to Jesus. As Barna concludes: "Gen Z remains refreshingly open to Jesus as an influence in their lives."[13] So why aren't they around? Turns out, they're staying away not because they're disinterested but because they're disillusioned. As the title of one Barna report points out: "Openness to Jesus Isn't the Problem—the Church Is."[14]

For example, during one of my Spruce Lake pastor-for-the-week residencies, I got a chance to get to know the counseling staff, most of whom were Gen Z college students (my daughter was one of them). These were all-in, sold-out Jesus followers who cared deeply about their faith. Yet, almost all of them indicated that they hadn't been very active in their church or even attended worship very often. The biggest reason? Church people.

One young woman said the problem was: "Church people don't follow Jesus. They say they do, but their actions don't match. They don't really love people that are different from them. Not because they don't agree with their lifestyle but because they won't even talk to them. I believe Jesus would talk to everybody." The real problem is that when it comes to faith in action, Gen Zers feel the church is too hypocritical. The research from Barna is clear: "Globally, teens do not see Christians as positively as they see Jesus."[15]

A question for your team to consider might be: *How do we bridge the gap between how the next gen sees Jesus and how they see Christians or the church?* Perhaps the answer is as simple as relationship. Don Everts and Doug Schaupp, in their book, *I Once Was Lost*, talk about the five thresholds of postmodern conversion based on their work with college students. What they found is that the first step, or threshold, is simply to trust a Christian. How does that happen? Through genuine friendship.

They're Drawn to Jesus's Mercy

Again, the next generation is open. "This rising generation is open and inclusive, seeking truth, authenticity and change. They are open to different perspectives, different faiths, and different cultures."[16] When it comes to Jesus, however, global teens and emerging adults seem to struggle with what it means to follow him. Perhaps this is a byproduct of the technology at their fingertips—collapsing the world into soundbites and memes that don't fully articulate any given cultural or theological concept.

They know that Jesus was crucified on a cross and performed miracles. "However, teens feel less sure that they can have a personal relationship with Jesus and that he is active in the world today." There is a glaring thirty-point gap between teens who identify as Christian (52 percent) and those who say they've made a personal commitment to Jesus (22 percent).[17] For many younger people, Jesus may be an important figure from the past but isn't necessarily active or alive in the present.

But where Gen Zers across the globe overwhelmingly agree (according to Barna survey categories) is that Jesus is merciful. "About half of all teens, across faith groups, describe Jesus as 'loving' (49 percent) and believe he offers hope to (46 percent) and cares about people (43 percent)."[18] While they may not believe in or understand the resurrection, they do admire Jesus as an historical figure who showed grace.

Perhaps there's an opportunity, through Jesus's mercy, to build bridges to deeper understanding. As Barna suggests: "There is room for a new kind of catechesis for today's teenagers, drawing them toward reverence of and relationship with the merciful Jesus they so admire."[19] What would that look like in your context? Maybe you can offer a mission or service opportunity that leans into mercy. Then, as you develop relationships, you can start to teach more about the real Jesus. You can color in the rest of the picture for them.

They're Looking for Truth

Face-to-face with Pontius Pilate (in John 18:37–38), Jesus told him, "Everyone on the side of truth listens to me." To that, Pilate famously retorted, "What is truth?" There is an existential crisis the next generation faces, and it has everything to do with truth. In a culture that has taught Gen Z that truth is relative or subjective, they are struggling to answer foundational questions of identity, morality, and ultimate meaning.

Gen Z is certainly obsessed with identity. But before casting stones, we must acknowledge that it's not just a generational thing; it's a humanity thing. We are wired to know and be known by God. As J. Warner Wallace puts it, "The Christian story is an identity story from start to finish."[20] But in a culture where self-identity is so malleable, it can create a lot of confusion.

Carl Trueman, in a 2022 talk titled "Obsession with Self-Identity, Sexuality, and Rewriting History," asserts that this stems from a shift from outward-facing to inward-turning, "expressive individualism."[21] For example, let's say I'm the son of a butcher in upstate New York in the late 1800s. My grandfather was a butcher, and his father, and so on. There is no identity crisis because I know exactly who I am: I'm a butcher. That's what our family does.

However, in 2025, I may be the son of a butcher, but that may not be who I feel I am or strive to be. I may be sick of dealing with animal carcasses and stuck day in and day out in the butcher shop. Through self-reflection and examination, I discover my true identity. Gender, sexuality, vocational affinity, etc., are all determined by each individual's lived truth. Trueman calls it an expressive individualism. It's the belief "that each person has a unique core of feeling and intuition that should unfold or be expressed if individuality is to be realized."[22] This inward turning isn't necessarily a bad thing in itself, but it does come with complications.

For Gen Z, morality is also a subjective, lived truth. A favorite phrase in our current cultural milieu is to "live your truth." A recent Barna report indicates that "nearly three in five Gen Z (57 percent) agree there are facts we can know about scientific questions but not religious or moral questions. Gen Z are also much more willing to believe what is morally right or wrong depends on what an individual believes (60 percent)."[23]

I'll also say that while subjective truth is important to Gen Z, it doesn't mean they're not looking for objective truth. I have a theory (based on what I've seen and heard from Gen Zers). There seems to be a kind of exhaustion teens and emerging adults are experiencing while trying to hold a seemingly unlimited number of personal truths in tension. When young people find the anchor of truth, Jesus Christ, they seem both relieved and energized. In all their mining for truth, once they hit paydirt, they can "be still" and know God (Ps. 46:10).

Churches need to understand that Gen Zers have a different starting point when it comes to truth—it's not necessarily better or worse; it's just different. In 2024, we had the chance to interview the aforementioned J. Warner Wallace for *The Reclaimed Leader* podcast (he's one of our favorites). Wallace writes books that use his expertise as a cold case homicide detective (he's often seen on *Dateline*) to say something true about God. In our most recent conversation, I asked him what he was seeing in the spiritual hunger of the next generation. He explained that back when he was a young adult, it was all about evidence: *Prove that the gospel is true.* But now, Gen Zers have a different starting point. Their attitude is: *Prove that the gospel is good.*

Truth for this generation is often proven in the doing. They certainly care about evidential, objective truth. But to what end is something true? Subjectively, how does truth show up in life and faith? How does it impact the world around us? They take seriously the words of James: "Do not merely listen to the word, and so deceive yourselves. Do what it says" (James 1:22). Gen Zers seem to be attracted to Christians who walk the talk and repulsed by those who don't.

They're Doing Life Differently

What's fascinating about Gen Zers is that they're both traditional and nonconformist in their values. They are "earnest, hardworking, and driven by conservative views of success regarding money, education, and career advancement" (like their boomer grandparents), and yet, they are "writing modern rules that favor liberal views on race, gender, identity, and sexuality."[24] And they care deeply about advocacy and justice around these topics. They don't just believe things—they want to do things to make a difference. This sounds a lot like the children of the 1960s.

But they are unlike their grandparents in that they're waiting much longer to get married or enter the workforce (partially due to job availability). They have no qualms about returning home to buy time (and cut expenses) as they navigate adult benchmarks. Due to delayed maturity, they find themselves dancing between extended adolescence and adulthood. They even have a name for it: *adulting*. When they do adult tasks (applying for a job, leasing an apartment, or paying their taxes), they are adulting. This implies they don't identify as adults but only with adult actions.

As Kara Powell, Jake Mulder, and Brad Griffin point out, adulthood for Gen Z is a bit of a paradox. It is delayed in some ways but accelerated in others. "On the one hand, their journey toward adulthood has sped up. On the other hand, it has slowed down."[25] They are coming of age faster biologically than previous generations and have had to deal with life circumstances with a maturity beyond their years.

The COVID-19 pandemic is a perfect example. Gen Zers experienced a "blip"—like in the Marvel Universe (a franchise they grew up with). In *Spider-Man: Far from Home*, half the population of the world disappeared and returned five years later, only to find that life kept going without them. They had to go through a time of adjustment upon their return to the world. Similarly, many (including my daughter) missed out on proms, homecomings, graduation ceremonies, sports, and many of the normal rites of passage. They had masks on for nearly two years and developed social anxiety when it was time to take them off.

Perhaps it's no surprise that one of the highest values of Gen Z is authenticity. It's about being who you really are—the version of you with your mask down. That's why hypocritical Christians are such a turnoff. Gen Zers believe in congruence between thought, word, and deed and will respect, if not celebrate, just about anyone they deem to be authentic.

And it's probably a big reason why they crave community. Gen Zers want to belong. They need analog touch in a digital world. Yes, they experience some sense of community via social media, but they much prefer if that connection leads to in-person community. They love it when "snaps" (Snapchat communications) turn into impromptu flag football games at the high school turf, lunches at the taco stand, or parties in the neighboring town. They're up for adventure and are hungry to be together. As Nancy Beach and Samantha Beach Kiley put it in their book *Next Sunday*, if churches could offer "authentic, vibrant, three-dimensional community, that would be deeply compelling if not irresistible" for Gen Zers.[26]

One of the most hopeful signs that came from *Growing Young* was that emerging adults, overwhelmingly, look for a warm church: hospitable, authentic, and welcoming. "As it turns out, *warm* is indeed the new *cool*."[27] If making a list of what they're looking for in a church, warmth is number one—and I think this is a huge myth buster. It's not artisan coffee. It's not dynamic preaching. It's belonging. It's community.

They're Digital in Their DNA

Make no mistake—these are the digital natives. "Today's teens [and young adults] are the first generation of consumers to have grown up in an entirely post-digital era."[28] They don't remember the world before smartphones, iPads, and on-demand digital content. It's a part of who they are. It seems like they "came out of the womb with the ability to pinch, swipe, and zoom."[29]

Digital technology is a seamless part of their lives. It's how they navigate the world around them. They're the multiscreen generation. They can be streaming Netflix on a TV, "snapping" a friend from summer camp on their phone, doing homework on their laptop using Google Drive, and checking the school lunch calendar on an iPad—all at the same time. Somehow, they can hold it all together.

It's also a big part of how they experience faith. They download and access spiritual content from their phones. One of our young adults who grew up in the church had a huge faith transformation in high school. We thought it happened through our confirmation program. It didn't. He told us he came upon a Christian TikTok account, and through it, he gave his life to Christ. "Teenagers and emerging adults can—and do—connect with everyone and learn about everything online."[30]

Digital technology has become a core element of how they learn. Have you been to your kids' or grandkids' classroom? They don't sit and listen to the teacher lecture for an hour. They learn in cohorts. They collaborate on assignments. They don't have chalkboards or textbooks. They have smart boards and Chromebooks. The way they learn is fundamentally different than previous generations.

All this screen time has made them incredibly savvy. In *Marketing to Gen Z*, Jeff Fromm and Angie Read talk about the incredible pressure marketers face trying to reach them. "Research conducted by Microsoft Corp. found the average attention span has decreased from twelve to eight seconds."[31] Eight seconds to convince a Gen Zer to buy. But that's not all. Marketing has to be friendly, authentic, consistent, humorous, compassionate, and secure—in eight seconds. Often, ads have to work without sound since many are scrolling on mute.

As you can imagine, this all has huge implications for church. For example, is your Sunday school model based on an educational model, lecture-based content, that no longer exists? If it is, you'll struggle to keep their attention, which will prevent biblical retention. Do you engage your young adults online? Do you have Snapchat to communicate with them? Do you point them to solid digital content? Or is all the content you give them based on being in the same room?

How Do We Start Translating?

The next generation is optimistic, excited about the future, and looking for their place in the world. They are, in my experience, hilarious, smart, and capable of more than they currently believe. As Asbury University president Kevin Brown pointed out, they just might be the cure to casual Christianity. Going forward, what do they need?

As *Growing Young* points out, they're trying to answer the three core questions of human experience: questions about identity, belonging, and purpose. "They are often what keep today's teenagers and emerging adults awake at night. *Who am I? Where do I fit? What difference do I make?*"[32] They need guidance to find the answers.

And yet, our churches are perfectly calibrated to give them information. But information isn't what they need (they have it all beneath their lock screens). What they need is interpretation and application. They need more than soundbites, reels, and memes. They need instruction on how to process that information into lifelong discipleship—belief into action. As Fromm and Read put it, "Gen Z is communicating faster than you can plan, learning faster than you can teach, and consuming faster than you can create. So, take a deep breath and stop trying to get it perfect. Instead, just get real."[33]

For Further Thought: Next Gen

- When was the last time you engaged with Gen Zers? What would it look like to have faith conversations with them?
- We looked at the generational differences between growing up Gen Z and growing up in previous generations, but what are the similarities? How can that provide some points of connection?
- What would it look like for your church to go all-in with the next generation?

Chapter Seven

CLOSING THE GAP WITH DISCIPLESHIP

This is what the Lord says: "Stand at the crossroads and look; ask for the ancient paths, ask where the good way is and walk in it, and you will find rest for your souls."
—JEREMIAH 6:16

In 2023, our family had a spring break vacation that didn't work out. We were trying to get our three kids on a trip to someplace warm. But due to conflicting schedules with school, sports, and work, three out of five of us couldn't go. My high schooler was probably the most let down since he was the one really pushing for a trip. Since we were the only ones available, my wife suggested we try and get away—just he and I—for a couple of days.

I did some quick math, cashed in hotel points, reserved a rental car, and followed the spring break migration from New Jersey to the sun-drenched shores of Florida (and I do mean sun-drenched; we had to bathe in aloe afterwards). We only had two full days in Orlando, so we did the beach one day and Universal Studios on the other.

What I'd failed to consider about going to Universal was that my son needed a riding buddy for the big roller coasters. Usually, he'd have his older sister to ride with, and I'd find a park bench and an ice cream sandwich. But not this time. On an already disappointing partial-family vacation, I didn't want to let him down. So I told him that whatever ride he wanted to go on, I was going to do it with him.

We rode the VelociCoaster, a roller coaster based on the Jurassic World franchise. It's a ride that boasts a top speed of seventy mph, a vertical climb of 155 feet (with an eighty-degree drop), and two launches (where the ride accelerates) across 4,700 feet of track. The description from the Orlando Informer says: "There are four inversions . . . a 360-degree barrel roll above water and a zero-gravity inverted stall that lasts for some one hundred feet. . . . All told, Universal promises a total of twelve seconds of airtime—an exhilarating amount of time for riders to be lifted out of their seats."[1] Yes, exhilarating. There are other words I would use to describe the experience as well.

On most modern, high-thrill coasters, there's a locking harness that lowers over your shoulders and buckles to the seat. Typically, it's tight enough to limit any movement. But not on the VelociCoaster. On this ride, there is no harness. The only restraint is a lap bar. *A lap bar.* At least six or seven times, it felt like that bar was barely keeping us from certain death as we hurled weightless through the twists and turns.

I'm not sure if it was my nerves or if something simply short-circuited in my brain, but when the ride came to a stop, all I could do was laugh. I looked over at my son, and he was laughing, too. That coaster put the thrill in thrill ride. Each part of the experience was unexpected. The speed. The double-launch (where you accelerate halfway through the ride). Each drop and weightless change of direction was a surprise. We both loved it.

The VelociCoaster brought a rush of joy I didn't see coming. As I surfed for movies on the chairback screen in front of me on the flight home, I kept thinking about how that experience was a lot like following Jesus. Discipleship is a thrill ride. As I'm led and fed by the Holy Spirit, each change of direction, each launch into the unknown, is a surprise. There are so many unexpected twists and turns. It's exhilarating and a bit terrifying. It's the adventure of a lifetime that brings so much joy.

As I made this connection, my very next thought was: *Why don't most Christians think about discipleship this way?* If I had to gauge the adventure level of most churchgoing Jesus followers, it'd probably look less like a roller coaster and more like a lazy river: predictable, slow, a bit boring, and marked by inactivity.

Maybe They Don't Know What It Means

In *The Princess Bride*, there's a memorable exchange between Vizzini and Inigo. Vizzini keeps saying the word "inconceivable" in response to the actions of the Man in Black (aka the hero, Westley). Finally, Inigo whirls around and says, "You keep using that word—I don't think it means what you think it means."[2]

Likewise, I think many churchgoers have a deficient view of discipleship and keep using that word without really understanding what it means. For many, especially "builders" in the mainline, discipleship is a faith-based combination of regular worship attendance and volunteerism. This is what following Jesus looks like. If you're not doing both, you're not really following. Sometimes, this leads them into an animosity toward younger generations because most of them don't engage in the same way. Exasperated, they say: *The young people should be taking over this ministry.* Or, as they hold their thirty-ninth annual chili dinner, they look around and ask: *Where are all the young people? Why aren't they helping out?*

To the credit of the "builders," they have an unmatched dedication to running the church. You can count on them. If they said they will do it, they will do it. They pledge their giving. They cut the grass. They have keys to the building. But there's a dark side to this when it comes to discipleship.

Years ago, a lifelong member (eighty-six years old) who volunteered in various capacities around the church suddenly fell ill and was unable to continue his church work. As a result, over a period of several weeks, he began to question whether or not he was right with God precisely because he felt he wasn't doing enough. *I do good works. Therefore, God loves me.* For him, discipleship was a form of volunteerism, and when he could no longer volunteer, he didn't know how keep following Jesus.

Younger generations can certainly struggle with this, too. But theirs is usually a different discipleship problem. Do you remember Trivial Pursuit, the board game from the 1980s? Each player had a game piece that looked like a pie with six triangular slices removed. The goal was to answer trivia questions and earn triangular pie slices in each of the six categories. If you filled them all and answered the final question correctly, you won the game.

Trivial Pursuit discipleship is treating faith as one slice (out of many) in one's life (work, friends, family, leisure). It's the compartmentalizing of discipleship—keeping it separated from the other slices. However, God's activity in our lives includes every slice of the pie. As Abraham Kuyper once put it, "There is not a square inch in the whole domain of our human existence over which Christ, who is sovereign over all, does not cry, 'Mine!'"[3] Discipleship, then, isn't relegated to church activity, but it necessarily includes the activity of everyday life.

Both the good works and Trivial Pursuit models of discipleship suffer the same deficiency: lack of a relationship with God. This may be at the heart of why it can be so difficult to revitalize churches. It's the hollowing out of the Christian faith. It's separating belief from relationship—or worse, that belief is the same thing as relationship.

In 1729, John Wesley, while attending Oxford University, started what became known as "the Holy Club"[4] with his brother Charles and their friends. The club had three components. First, they had to be orthodox in their belief (adhere to creeds and confessions). Second, they had to do good works. Third, they had to participate in religious activity (attend worship and prayer services multiple times a week). "Yet in spite of this extraordinary combination of orthodoxy, philanthropy, and piety, John Wesley later reckoned that he was not a Christian at all at the time."[5] The reason? The lack of relationship. It wasn't until 1738, when he "visited a Moravian meeting in Aldersgate Street, East London," that everything changed. As someone read Martin Luther's preface to his commentary on Romans, "a personal faith was born in Wesley's heart. He wrote in his journal: 'I felt my heart strangely warmed.'"[6]

Why Hearts Are Still Cold

The language of spirituality has become pervasive in contemporary US culture. Talk of spiritual wholeness and wellness, once relegated to Sunday morning sermons, can be found in health clubs, spas, boardrooms, and magazine covers. Whenever pollsters ask about faith, it seems that most Americans overwhelmingly affirm that they believe in God, pray to God, and share "testimonials of personal encounters with God,"[7] even as participation in traditional religious activity in the United States continues to decline. Simply put, religious institutions are no longer the places where people are getting all (or any) of their spiritual information. Many Americans have become skeptical of religious institutions and have turned to a burgeoning "spirituality industry" to meet their needs.

Over the last few decades, this "spirituality industry" (a conglomeration of religion, philosophy, perceived supernatural phenomena, psychic readings, and self-help psychology) has flooded popular culture with books, movies, television programs, seminars, and media personalities, all of which promise answers to the fundamental questions of all things "spiritual." Sociologist Robert Wuthnow, in his book *After Heaven: Spirituality in America since the 1950s*, argues that all of this is a sign of a profound change in US spirituality that has taken place in the last half of the twentieth century: a traditional spirituality of dwelling (congregations, denominations, and neighborhoods) has given way to a new spirituality of seeking. Popular notions of spiritual experience (such as angels, spirit guides, and near-death experiences) and the development of the inner self are examples of a growing seeker-oriented spirituality that places a premium on individual experience.

Spirituality, framed in this way, is a journey more than it is a destination. In Peter Rollins's book *How (Not) to Speak of God*, he calls this one of the fundamental differences between modernity and post-modernity. In modernity, he argues, one becomes a Christian, joins a church, and is saved (spirituality of dwelling). In post-modernity, one is becoming a Christian and is being saved (spiritually of seeking). Rollins, as well as most Americans, believes (to one degree or another) that God is the known unknown, that no human ideology can claim a monopoly on understanding God. Consequently, many people consider themselves to be spiritual rather than religious, and they refrain from committing to any one set of values or doctrines. Instead, they become hunters and gatherers for spiritual information, assemble their beliefs in piecemeal fashion, and engage in and learn from anything that falls under the spirituality umbrella.

What do we mean when we talk about spiritual formation, or discipleship? In his book *Renovation of the Heart*, Dallas Willard says that spiritual formation generally refers to "the process by which the human spirit or will is given a definite 'form' or character."[8] This is the journey that most Americans believe they are undertaking as spiritual beings—the individual quest for fulfillment through what we have broadly defined as spirituality. But is this what we mean by Christian spiritual formation? Or is Christian spirituality a different animal altogether?

The answer is complicated. Christian practice in the United States has been profoundly influenced by these changing trends in spirituality, as Christianity has tried to remain competitive in the "spiritual marketplace of ideas" (Christian entertainment, prosperity theology, a focus on technology, and a greater emphasis on finding truth in non-Christian religions). As a result, the church has become, to a large degree, just one of many purveyors of spiritual goods and services designed to enhance one's personal spiritual journey.

For example, there are two phenomena that are byproducts of this reality: church shopping and church hopping. The first involves a desire to find a church where one's spiritual needs can be met, while the second involves avoiding commitment in favor of a broader-based sense of community. The making of meaning for these Christians is synthesized not only from Scripture but from popular culture as well. While Christian worship and prayer is a big part of their life, they derive many of their beliefs from movies, music, and television.

Many Christians have seen this pervasiveness of "secular spirituality" as a good thing for the church. It's a sign of the world's insatiable hunger for truth that will eventually lead them to Jesus Christ. Perhaps this is true. But there is a very real danger that the Christian notions of spirituality and spiritual formation have been tainted by popular culture. Is Christian spiritual formation primarily about the individual journey of the spiritual self? Not exactly. Spiritual formation, for the Christian, is not focused on the self but on the person of Jesus Christ. It is "secular spiritual formation" in reverse—it focuses on God so that God can form the self. As Willard puts it, "spiritual formation for the Christian basically refers to the Spirit-driven process of forming the inner world of the human self in such a way that it becomes like the inner being of Christ himself."[9] It is a spiritual journey with an end in mind: the loss of self—Christlikeness. It is a constant shaping and reshaping of the human self more and more into the image of Christ. According to Willard, "This reshaping is the basic meaning of spiritual formation in the Christian tradition."[10] But how does this reshaping take place?

Spiritual formation, throughout the biblical witness, is often described as the decision (both individual and communal) to turn toward God. This turning is always a matter of the heart. As disciples of Jesus Christ, we are called to follow the way of righteousness, to lose ourselves in Christ, and to allow ourselves to be shaped by God. We must willingly become "living sacrifice[s], holy and acceptable to God" (Rom. 12:1 ESV), allowing ourselves to be transformed by the renewing of our minds. But, spiritual mind renewal doesn't mean that our faith should be trapped there.

Discipleship Is Apprenticeship

As I mentioned earlier, perhaps the biggest obstacle to overcome is that many churchgoers think discipleship is primarily about knowledge. They see it like a tiered college course system: *I go from the 101 to the 201 to the 301 levels as I mature as a Christian.* Of course, there's nothing wrong with knowledge, but there is something wrong with thinking that knowledge, in itself, is the way to follow Jesus. Why? Because knowledge alone doesn't produce results.

For example, I know a lot about nutrition. But when I go out to eat, I'll pick the cheeseburger and fries over a salad nine times out of ten. It's not that I don't know what's better for me—I'm instead choosing gratification. Take seminary, for instance. What's the running joke? People call it "cemetery" instead of "seminary" because it has a reputation for killing faith. Knowledge only matters when it's reflected in the doing.

As we've touched on already, learning is cemented by doing. Think Mr. Miagi from *The Karate Kid*. The learning is in the muscle memory: sand the floor; wax on, wax off; paint the fence. Discipleship is an apprenticeship program during which we learn alongside a mentor and eventually do it ourselves. It's knowledge and action. We learn each lesson by doing. John Mark Comer, in his book *Practicing the Way*, reminds us of the three goals of discipleship (at the time of Jesus): (1) to be with your rabbi (spend time with Jesus), (2) to become like your rabbi (allow Jesus to form you through the Holy Spirit), and (3) to do as your rabbi did (carry on the *Missio Dei* in community).[11]

Two fundamental questions of discipleship are: *Who am I following? Who am I becoming as a result?* We're all following someone (or something). This is consciously and subconsciously shaping us. When I lived in Los Angeles, California, as a ninth grader, I played water polo, listened to bands like Depeche Mode, and wore Maui and Sons surfer shirts. But when I lived in East Stroudsburg, Pennsylvania, as a tenth grader, I played football, listened to bands like Guns N' Roses, and wore lots of flannel. Why? Because who I became was impacted by who I spent time with. *How do I make room for the Holy Spirit to form me into the person God called and created me to be?*

Discipleship Doesn't Happen by Accident

Over the last two years, I've been on a journey toward better health. Once I hit fifty, the thought of my own mortality, let's say, felt a bit more urgent. While I wouldn't consider myself an expert, there is a fundamental truth to becoming more fit: it doesn't happen by accident. I didn't wake up one day, look at myself in the mirror and say, "Wow, look at this—I dropped thirty pounds and have six-pack abs! I don't know what happened; this is amazing!" What I learned quickly in this journey is that you don't just drift into health (actually, the opposite is true). It takes a regimen of diet and exercise. It takes intention. (It should be noted that I still don't have six-pack abs.)

Of course, this is common sense. Yet, most churches are functioning with no intentional strategy for discipleship. They just hope it happens as a result of proximity and programs. *If we have Bible studies, service opportunities, retreats, events, etc., they will grow in their faith.* Hope is a wonderful thing, but it's not a very effective strategy. Jesus didn't call his disciples and hope they drifted into faith. He was incredibly intentional. He taught, interpreted, and helped them apply the lessons they learned through their shared experiences. His call to "make disciples of all nations" (Matt. 28:19) is a call to do something intentional.

Before we jump into developing the discipleship strategy of your church, we must acknowledge a tension we're trying to hold together. Discipleship is a high-touch enterprise. It's developed in relationship. As we've discussed, discipleship isn't just knowledge—it's knowledge and action. It's cemented in the doing. Personal mentoring is a critical component. After all, disciples are handcrafted, not mass-produced. But how do you scale personal mentoring for an entire church?

Discipleship Pathways

How should we approach discipleship? Psalm 1 is a good place to start, as it lays out the spiritual journey as the choice between two ways: the way of the righteous and the way of the wicked. Whoever follows the way of the righteous, "That person is like a tree planted by streams of water . . . whatever they do prospers" (v. 3). But "not so the wicked!" (v. 4). How do we know the way of the righteous? By following Jesus, who told us, "I am the way, the truth, and the life. No one comes to the Father except through me" (John 14:6 ESV).

Have you ever been geocaching? It's kind of a global treasure hunt. "Over three million cleverly hidden containers called geocaches are hidden all over the world just waiting to be found."[12] To join the hunt, most sign up for a geocaching club, download an app, and select a cache. Then they receive GPS coordinates, and the search begins. All you need is a sense of adventure and a reliable GPS (most use their phones).

Let's say, however, you don't have a smartphone or working GPS device. Imagine you have to simply read the latitude and longitude on a physical map to find the cache. Maybe the hardcore geocachers would love it, but it would probably weed out most of the others. Why? Because after a while, you'll hit a ravine or a mountain that you weren't prepared for. Or the forest may be too thick for you to get your bearings. *Are we going west right now? I can't see where the Sun is.* Or, *My compass says we need to go north, but there's a river that's a quarter-mile across.* The whole adventure will eventually become a headache, and you'll probably decide to stop following.

In a way, this is what it's like to follow Jesus. Discipleship is an adventure. If you follow the coordinates (aka the leading of the Holy Spirit), you'll find the millions of hidden treasures God has in store. But, just like geocaching, if you don't have a reliable GPS, it won't take long before discouragement sets in. If the strategy of your church is simply to hope people grow as disciples of Jesus Christ, it's kind of like asking them to find their way through the woods with a hand-drawn map on a napkin.

For example, Dave and his wife, Jill, decide it's time to try church again. With all the craziness happening in the world, it seems like getting reconnected with God (and getting their third- and fifth-grade daughters to learn about Jesus) would be good for them. So they do a quick Google search for churches in their area with Sunday school for kids. Your church pops up. Does your website help them take a step? Is there a link to online worship so they can see what the church is like? Is there a contact form? Is there a tab for "I'm New Here" with a FAQ section?

After watching your online service, they feel it warrants an in-person visit. They arrive at your door, a bit nervous, but with a sense of hope. Do they know where to go? Do they know where to take their kids? Are there people greeting them as they come in? Once they're settled, the service begins with ten minutes of announcements. Is everything explained for newcomers? Are there opportunities for them to connect? When it comes time for the sermon, they discover that it's part seven of a sermon series on Nehemiah. Will they be able to track with the message? Are they afraid they've missed too much and tune out? After the service, they collect their kids and head back home. Is there any follow-up with some next steps?

Dave, Jill, and their daughters enjoyed the experience enough to come back. They've now become regulars (once or twice a month) for about six months. Jill feels like she's ready to go deeper in her faith. Does she know what opportunities are available? Does she know what step to take next? She heard something about a women's circle gathering in the library on Wednesdays. She's not comfortable just showing up, and she isn't sure it's what she's looking for.

Clarity is the key to following. Sadly, most of our churches are unclear about how to take a step toward Jesus (wherever you are in your faith). Notice that in Dave and Jill's journey from Google search to engaged attenders, there were many steps at which they could've become confused and disengaged. Without clarity, it makes it harder to follow.

We need to cultivate a discipleship pathway for people like Dave and Jill, a curated series of logical, clear steps toward Jesus. I first heard the language of pathways when I interviewed the late Tony Morgan of The Unstuck Group on *The Reclaimed Leader* podcast in 2018. He talked about the difference between programs and pathways. Instead of a curated series of steps, programs have very little connection with one another. Often, they are competing for attention and resources, fostering siloed ministry instead of synergetic ministry. Programs create clutter, but pathways create clarity. "We believe church programs should not work in competition with each other, but work as steps to move people down a relational path to where we want them to go."[13] As Jeremiah 6:16 puts it, "This is what the Lord says: 'Stand at the crossroads and look; ask for the ancient paths, ask where the good way is, and walk in it, and you will find rest for your souls.'"

The best strategy for discipling Dave, Jill, and their family is to have personal mentors assigned to them. It's Jesus's model. If you're a small church, you have a huge advantage because you can actually do it. But this strategy is really difficult to scale. Once you get past a few dozen people, it's hard to keep up. So we try to create opportunities for mentoring to happen, for spiritual friendships to form, and for the Jills and Daves to discover their pathway toward Jesus. We may not have the resources to assign them a personal mentor, but we can get them into a small group where they are connected and shepherded.

It's like sightseeing in New York City. Since I live within an hour of Manhattan, I've pretty much done the tourist stuff. When I go, I'm not interested in seeing everything, but I want to see a couple strategic sights—skating in Central Park and enjoying frozen hot chocolate at Serendipity 3 on the Upper East Side. I could take a tour of the city, but the bus goes to all the sights and it takes me all day. Then I don't get to spend enough time where I want to be. But a personalized (curated) tour meets my needs. Let's say I have a few friends who want to do this with me. Now we've created memories that will last a lifetime. This is what we hope the small group pathway accomplishes.

We are great at potlucks and programs. But we're terrible at pathways. Pathways are what we need to help deliver spiritual formation at scale (while making it relational). Pathways will necessarily include programs. The difference is that the programs are strung together in a series of intentional steps (we'll take a look at an example at the end of the chapter). You will have multiple pathways depending on where people are in their faith journey. This leads to the need for an overarching structure, or framework, for it all. Like in geocaching, you need the coordinates for the cache, but you also need the app that organizes all the caches and coordinates.

Developing the Framework (the Home Satellite Model)

Over twenty years ago, Andy Stanley and North Point Community Church developed the "foyer to kitchen" strategy as a framework to help people take a step. In *Creating Community*, Stanley and Bill Willits explain, "Like the room of a house, the environments of the church function for different purposes to help people connect"[14] (see Figure 7.1). It begins with the "foyer"—the formal entry point where you welcome guests. Friends and family come in through the garage or side door. But guests get the red carpet. When you welcome guests, you're "sensitive to their needs and desires."[15] At North Point, the "foyer" is primarily their worship gatherings—"large environments designed to change people's minds about church."[16] Their goal is to get guests to come back and eventually invite them into the "living room."

The "living room" is designed for people to get to know each other. "[It is] usually arranged in such a way that it allows people to casually connect . . . where guests begin to feel like *friends*."[17] At North Point, "living room" environments are medium-sized discussion groups or special affinity group gatherings. The goal is to "change people's minds about connecting"[18] to make them want more of it. The desired outcome is that they would want to come to the "kitchen table."

The "kitchen table" is the small group environments at North Point. "[It's] where people share their experiences, discuss important questions, and enjoy meals . . . where close friends begin to feel more like *family*."[19] The goal is to "change people's minds about their priorities"—to align more and more with God's will. In other words, the "kitchen table" is their discipleship delivery system.

The strength of the "foyer to kitchen" framework is that it's based on relationships. It's always about helping people take a step, not about programs (although programs do play a key role). After I heard Andy Stanley talk about this model, I brought it back to our team. Not only did we integrate it, but it has become a fundamental part of our successful discipleship strategy.

In recent years, we reimagined this model in a way that acknowledges two important truths about discipleship. The first is that small groups alone aren't the discipleship strategy; they're only part of it. *Everything* is the discipleship strategy. From stranger in the "neighborhood" to guest in the "foyer" to friend in the "living room" to family at the "kitchen table," it's all part of the journey of following Jesus.

Discipleship isn't always linear. That's why our adapted model looks like satellites traveling around the Earth. In the center is the mission, with the "neighborhood," "foyer," "living room," and "kitchen table" around it. We added the "neighborhood" category because we needed a way to create pathways for the "pre-guest" phase. This is what many churches call outreach or evangelism (which we'll tackle in the next chapter).

This framework is a container for all the discipleship pathways we create. For example, Christmas is the biggest outreach opportunity of the year (especially for young families). It used to be Christmas and Easter, but no more. Easter is for Christians. Christmas is for culture. Of course, it's also for Christians, but you get what I mean. Just about everyone celebrates Christmas in some way. Even my Jewish uncle celebrates it—for him, it's about family and friends and connection. So how do we leverage the cultural love for Christmas as a relational touch point with young families in our area? Well, every year, we create a pathway designed to bring them from the "neighborhood" to the "foyer" and hopefully further.

Imagine a pathway as a funnel (wider at the top and narrower at the bottom). As you invite people to take steps toward Jesus, not everyone will come with you. And that's okay. It happened to Jesus, too. The following is what our Christmas pathway looks like for young families we're trying to reach (see Figure 7.2). First, we host a communitywide event called Christmas on the Hill. It's a low-risk, high-fun, free event that is optimized for young families: tree lighting, firepits, s'mores, cookies, hot chocolate, photos with Santa, Christmas crafts, and live music. We run ads to draw attention to it, but mostly, we empower our own young families to invite other young families who don't attend church.

Right before the tree lighting, we'll have a child read Luke 2:1–14 (like Linus in the *Peanuts* cartoons). Before we lose their attention, we'll invite them to the next step in the pathway: our Christmas Eve family service with glowstick candle lighting. We say something like, *If you love this, you'll love our Christmas Eve service designed just for your family.* They'll get reminder postcards on their way out. "Neighborhood" to "foyer."

Then, on Christmas Eve, we'll announce opportunities coming up in January. Typically, we'll have a new round of small groups beginning. They'll be invited, but many will still be intimidated at this step. So there'll be other, less threatening options like spaghetti dinners or easy volunteer opportunities. This next step in the pathway is typically a fellowship step (that's how we define the "living room," programmatically).

This Christmas pathway is one of many discipleship pathways occurring across the life of the church for all ages and stages. The framework houses all the geocaching locations in one place so we can make sure they are well-organized and fully supported.

For Further Thought: Discipleship

- How are programs preventing you from getting clarity on your discipleship model?
- What would it look like to start thinking in terms of discipleship pathways or next steps? What steps could you offer already? What would need to be developed?
- How can you reawaken a sense of adventure in discipleship?

Figure 7.1. Discipleship Model

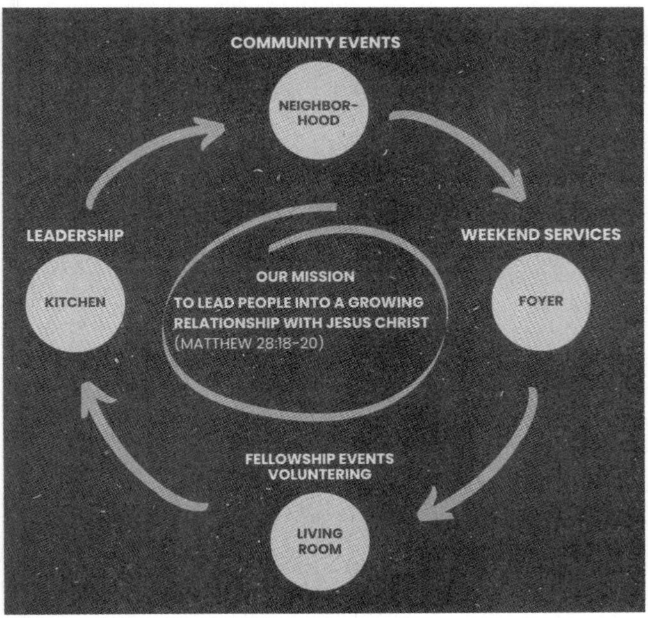

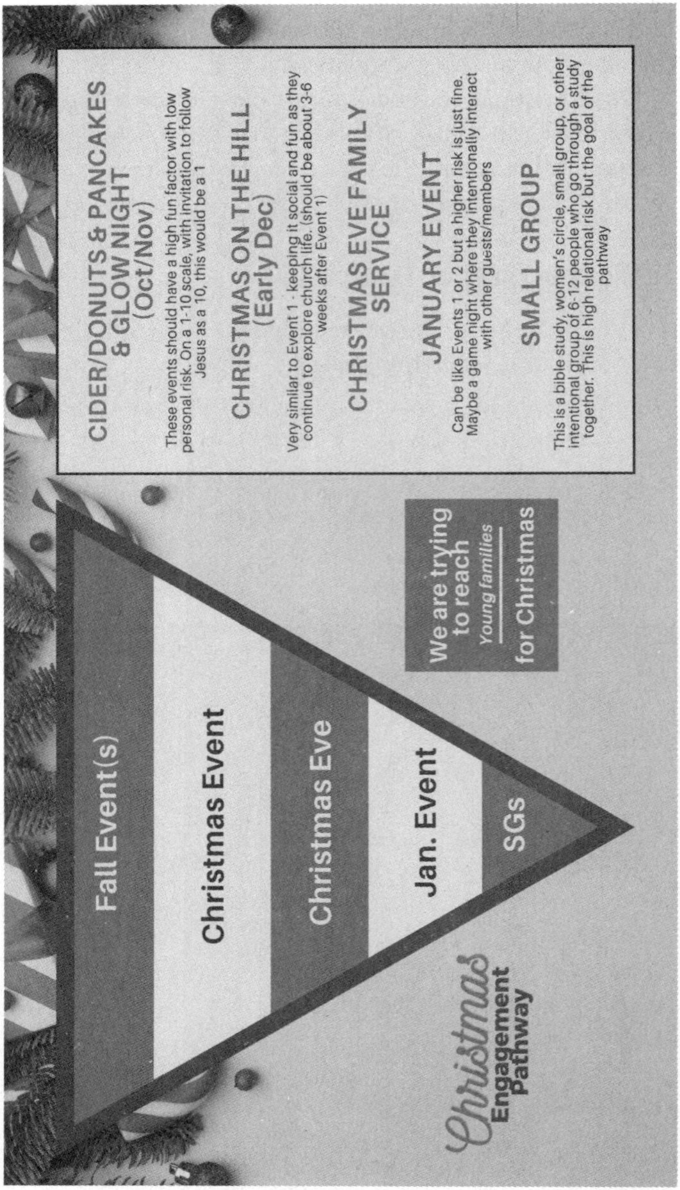

Figure 7.2. Christmas Pathway

Chapter Eight

CLOSING THE GAP WITH EVANGELISM

All my life I have been searching for that crazy, missing part. And with one touch, you just rolled away the stone that held my heart.

—KEITH GREEN, "UNTIL YOUR LOVE BROKE THRU"

Peter was a fair-haired eleven-year-old from the suburbs of Philadelphia. I vividly remember him and the Phillies baseball cap he wore every day. He was one of the eight kids I had in my cabin as a first-week, first-time camp counselor. I'd only been a Christian for three or four days, and the world still felt a bit like Dorothy landing in Oz. It went from black-and-white to technicolor in an instant. I was still trying to take it all in.

I had some first-day counselor jitters, but overall, leadership suited me. It felt natural—even fun. In many ways, as I led the kids from activity to activity and walked the line between goofy friend and responsible adult, I felt like my true self for the first time. The problem was Bible study. It was my daily dose of anxiety—not because of the Bible itself (I was excited to learn), but because I was completely over my skis when I had to teach it. I mean, I'd never read it. Every day felt like cramming for a test.

Every time the kids had a question, I'd do my best to answer, but invariably, I would end up saying something like: *I'm new at this, too, and I don't really know the answer yet, but I know whom to ask.* Then I'd bend the ear of any other counselor I could successfully corner and get back to the kids with some kind of answer. All I really had—all I really knew—was my story. At the end of the week, one of the kids asked how I became a Christian. That kid was Peter.

Peter had a lot of questions about Jesus. Honestly, I felt like the man born blind in John 9:25. He'd ask things, and I didn't really know how to answer them except with: *One thing I do know: I was blind, but now I see!* But, at Peter's request, I shared my testimony. After I shared it, Peter asked: "Can I accept Jesus, too?" I was completely unprepared for this, but it was a question I knew the answer to. "Yes, Peter. You can."

I asked if anyone else wanted to accept Jesus, and all the kids in the cabin said yes. So I did what Craig did with me on that mountaintop a few days prior. I led them in a prayer to put their faith in Jesus. I'm not great at memorization, but that prayer was burned into my brain. Together, all those kids in the first week accepted Jesus as their Lord and Savior.

Here's the crazy part: it happened again the second week. And the third. It happened all summer. Each week, I would tell my story. I would say about 80 percent of the kids in my cabin (six or seven a week) put their faith in Jesus. It was the most successful ministry of my life, and I was the least equipped for it. Maybe that's right where God wanted me. Before I had my ministry stories and bag of tricks, before I discovered *Mere Christianity* and *More Than a Carpenter*, I had to depend on God for every answer and in every situation. My ignorance led to incredible dependence. I think there's something to that.

Obviously, I don't think ignorance is the goal. I believe that reading and studying the Bible, learning theology, etc., is a critical part of the faith toolkit. As 1 Peter 3:15 tells us, "But in your hearts revere Christ as Lord. Always be prepared to give an answer to everyone who asks you to give the reason for the hope you have." But let's not forget the rest of verse 15 and the continuation of thought in verse 16 (because most evangelists do): "But do this with gentleness and respect, keeping a clear conscience, so that those who speak maliciously against your good behavior in Christ may be ashamed of their slander." Do it with gentleness and respect. The goal isn't ignorance, but dependence. If I can fully lean on God as I engage in ministry, it puts me in the correct posture (humility and grace) to share the gospel.

"Evangelism" is a word that has a ton of baggage. You (or your congregation) may even wince at that word. I suspect it has to do with heavy-handedness and using the Bible as a blunt-instrument, gospel-tract style of delivery that so often happens even with the most well-meaning Christians. It's the absence of gentleness and respect that repels instead of attracts people to Jesus.

Case in point, my first experience with evangelism was in seventh grade. My friend David, one day after science lab, handed me a little illustrated booklet. I'd never seen a gospel tract before, so I had no idea what I was in for—but wow, did it throw me. It was all about the dangers of rock 'n' roll music. I remember getting to the last page, where the unsuspecting teenager is literally possessed because they listened to the devil's music. The story (and the way it was illustrated) freaked me out, and not in a good way. It didn't point me to Jesus at all. It was just disturbing and scary. It had the effect of a horror movie—I just wanted to look away. I never spoke to David again.

My second evangelism experience was different. About a year later, I was with my mom at the Glendale United Methodist Church in California. No, we weren't churchgoers, but she ran the preschool connected to it. Since it was summer vacation, I often had to go to work with her so I wouldn't be home by myself. Most of the time, I would just shoot hoops in the church gym or sit and read in the preschool lunchroom.

On this particular day, the church was preparing for its annual Vacation Bible School. My mother broke the news to me that she (and therefore, I) had to be there to help run logistics. She suggested that I jump in with the teenage group for the week. I was not happy and wasn't having it. It was then that the head of VBS, Agnus Sayles, popped in the room and asked if I'd be her assistant for the week, to help her prepare snacks and other various tasks. It wasn't the first time I'd met Agnus. She clearly knew I had a spiritual wall up, but she saw an opportunity to invite me in (with gentleness and respect).

My experience with Agnus planted a seed. We didn't talk about Jesus. We didn't talk about the Bible or what the other kids were learning. She just asked me questions. She got to know me on my terms. She didn't seem to have an agenda for me (I would've sniffed that out). Do you know what that did? It helped me to trust a Christian (that first threshold). It was this trust that played a part in me trusting Craig on that mountaintop. Evangelism, at its heart, is an invitation. It's an invitation to relationship.

Evangelism is "a modified transliteration of the Greek word *euangelion*,"[1] which is a compound word meaning "good news." An evangelist is a messenger of this news, a messenger like Jesus, who, in his first message to the people around him, declared: "The kingdom of God has come near. Repent and believe the good news" (Mark 1:15)! This news isn't vague. It isn't hope in general. It's specifically that God's salvation is made possible and available to all through the life, death, and resurrection of Jesus Christ. It's God's impossible "yes" of grace in spite of our reality of sin. This salvation "is holistic, even cosmic in scope"[2] as God promises to make all things new.

"The Greek word *euangelizo* means 'to gospelize,' to tell people the good news about what Jesus did for us, and in the book of Acts literally everyone in the early church does it."[3] It's our divinely appointed mission to go into the world and make disciples. It's not relegated to clergy or professional staff. Congregations must be empowered and equipped to evangelize with gentleness and respect. The time is right now.

The Opportunity Is Real

On January 2, 2023, the Buffalo Bills played their week-seventeen game at the Cincinnati Bengals. Early in the game, after a routine tackle, Bills defensive back Damar Hamlin fell to the ground after suffering cardiac arrest. As he lay motionless on the field, "He was given medical treatment, including CPR, on the field for nearly twenty minutes before being taken in an ambulance to the University of Cincinnati Medical Center."[4]

My teenage son and I had watched a lot of games together and had seen a lot of injuries. But this was different. What made it so different was the reaction of the players and coaches. Many were crying, praying, and comforting one another. As we watched the events unfold, we decided to do something we'd never done before, at least while watching a football game: we prayed.

We weren't alone. In the ensuing minutes, we were amazed as sportscasters, newscasters, and TV personalities all exhorted people to pray for Damar. In fact, "All thirty-two NFL teams [included] 'Pray for Damar' on their Twitter avatars. ESPN's Dan Orlovsky prayed for the Buffalo Bills' safety on live TV. Countless fans and other concerned observers said on social media they were praying, and dozens linked arms outside his Cincinnati hospital."[5] When Hamlin eventually recovered, many publicly credited God and the power of prayer.

That same year, the "He Gets Us" campaign gained national attention when it aired commercials during the Super Bowl. "The ads featured a number of images leading to simple punchlines: 'Jesus didn't want us to act like adults' and 'Jesus loved the people we hate.' The reminders to have childlike faith and to love your enemies were designed to make viewers stop and think, with messages tailored to a skeptical secular audience that is accustomed to writing him off."[6] Despite criticism from Christians about reducing Jesus to a series of soundbites, the Lerma Agency, who runs the campaign, indicates that the ads have engaged 4.8 million website users and 1.4 billion video views.[7] Moreover, tens of thousands of people have requested prayer and have connected with "one of the twenty thousand churches that have partnered with 'He Gets Us.'"[8]

And then there's *Jesus Revolution*, a 2023 film that told the true story of Chuck Smith, Lonnie Frisbee, and Calvary Chapel in Costa Mesa, California, in the early 1970s. According to box office numbers, it smashed expectations, grossing over $15 million in its opening weekend and over $54 million worldwide since its release.[9] *Fifty-four million*. Was it simply nostalgia? Or was it something more? Add the Asbury University outpouring of that same year, and all of it paints a clear picture: people are hungry for Jesus in unprecedented numbers.

Outpouring at Tower Hill

It feels like the US church is perfectly poised for or even experiencing revival. That's what it's felt like at Tower Hill church. But immediately after saying "revival," there's a part of me that wants to reel it back in, to play it safe. Not because I don't want it, but because I'm afraid of being disappointed, looking foolish if I'm wrong, or mislabeling it. Maybe the approach at Asbury is a better one. What I've been seeing in front of me has been a kind of outpouring of the Holy Spirit.

In the last four years, since the COVID-19 restrictions eased in 2021, Tower Hill church has experienced revival firsthand. The most obvious place to start is with the sheer numbers of people engaging in the life of the church. Just over the last three years, we've grown by three hundred attendees per week. In Christmas 2024, we saw 3,003 people join us for worship (with over one thousand at one service in a sanctuary that seats seven hundred). For us, this growth is just insane.

While we'd been growing consistently since 2012, the real jump in numbers was a direct result of our online presence during the pandemic. Like most churches, we didn't start streaming until we had to. It was really bad. I can't even watch the old recordings. But we engaged a ton of people, especially a large number of local Catholics whose churches didn't offer online worship.

It wasn't just worship, either. In March 2020, I sent an email to our elders indicating a preliminary plan to cancel in-person worship on Sunday (and indefinitely), according to state guidelines. I also indicated in the email that, in a few days, I would be starting a daily Facebook devotional that was to begin at 10:10 a.m. I didn't even know what it was going to be about; I just felt the need to put out some life-giving content to battle the incessant doomscrolling and toilet paper hoarding that was going on. Why 10:10 a.m.? Because, in John 10:10, Jesus reminds us, "I have come that they may have life, and have it to the full." We all needed a reminder of life.

Between worship streaming and daily engagement through the devotional, our online impact was felt across our area. To this day, I still run into people I've never met who greet me by name and say, *Hey, we watched you during the pandemic.* Sure, many of them never engaged with us after things returned to normal (whatever that is), but many of them did. The result of all that online engagement had an impact on our in-person attendance.

By the time 2021 ended, we had 150 new members join (almost all of whom joined us online first). Many of them hadn't stepped foot in the church until they signed up for the new member class. (That's when we realized that online isn't a secondary ministry; it's a primary ministry and a new front door to the church.) But let's be clear: evangelism isn't just about increased attendance. There are a lot of ways to generate a crowd (which aren't always good or healthy). The real question is: Is the crowd becoming a congregation? Is there spiritual connection, engagement, and growth? Are people's hearts turning toward Jesus? Is evangelism happening? The answer, in our case, has been an unequivocal yes.

Between 2021 and 2024, we had more adult baptisms than in all the prior seventy-five-plus years of the church combined (I couldn't find the stats from before 1949). In that same time frame, our small group participation tripled. But it's more than that. It's story after story of people finding Jesus. It's the skeptical, the jaded, and the cynical drawing near to him. It's about lifelong Christians experiencing an awakening in their faith. It's about God doing what only God can do.

We're not a warehouse megachurch (that's not a slam, just a statement). We are definitely, uniquely us. We aren't the "greatest show on Earth" every week. We're intentionally not the attractional model of church in that way—we're not trying to put on a perfect production. We didn't jettison our traditional worship. We don't have artisan coffee. We still have a building that looks like a 1950s, colonial-style church (although we've worked hard to renovate our environment inside). We're just a regular church that decided to evangelize, to speak the wonders of God in the language of the culture around us. It worked. It worked largely because of the cultural climate we're living in.

The Starving and Allergic

I believe we're experiencing the biggest evangelism opportunity of our lifetime. People are starving for connection with God and with one another. People are looking for belonging and meaning (because they're wired that way). Global political upheaval, financial stress, social media, bad news after bad news after bad news. They are desperate for *euangelion*.

However, if that's true, then why aren't starving people coming to the table to eat? Why aren't they flocking to churches, fork in hand, to (as Psalm 34:8 encourages) "taste and see that the Lord is good"? As we discussed in Chapter Five, God is the one who feeds people, but our job is to set the table. It's a partnership. Sometimes, they don't come to the table because the table setting isn't very appealing (poor gospel translation). But other times, it's something much worse. Sometimes they are so scarred from bad evangelism that they've developed allergies to the meal.

For example, I was doing a church consultation near Bentonville, Arkansas, and went into town to check out their annual bike festival (pedal, not motor—big mountain-biking area). A young couple was handing out postcards to the crowd. They smiled warmly as they handed me a card and invited me to church. My first reaction was very positive, and I thought, *That's so cool; this church must really be reaching people.* But when I read the card a few minutes later, I nearly fell over.

It said, "Why Live Like You Won't Die?" When I flipped it over, it started with: "We all have an appointment with death." Then it went on a rant about how our sin condemns us to an eternity in hell. At the end, there was an invitation to put my faith in Jesus. There was nothing on the card I disagreed with theologically, but if I were a seeker, it would have repelled me from the gospel (like it did in middle school). It was so "cringe" (as my kids say). I am allergic to this style of evangelism. This means I will always walk away from this kind of table that is being set.

Churches aren't perfect. But if evangelism is about power and coercion, I'm out. Evangelism (and church revitalization, for that matter) isn't about getting more people to attend or making your programs more successful. That's not what we mean when we talk about reaching people. It's about open-handed, genuine relationship in which you want to lead hungry people to Jesus. You meet them where they are, allergies and all, and help them feel safe at the table.

If you've ever been out to eat with a friend or family member who has a food allergy, you learn a lot about what makes them feel safe. They have a lot of questions to determine what they can or can't have from the menu, or if accommodations can be made. If they're satisfied with the answers, they feel safe at the table and can enjoy the meal. If they don't, they just won't eat. They'd rather go hungry than risk inflammation.

In a similar way, people have baggage (allergies) with church, especially when it comes to evangelism. While we must focus on what to do, it may be just as important to focus on what not to do. Maybe a way to frame it is to say: evangelism is an invitation to invest in a relationship in the direction of Jesus. Evangelism is about genuine, incarnational friendship.

Evangelism Is Friendship

If my posture for evangelism is gentleness and respect born out of humility and grace, then I'm ready to share the gospel. But what does that look like? It looks like friendship. In 2022, I was speaking at a conference in Washington, DC. Before I left the hotel room that morning, I flipped on the TV. *Good Morning America* was on. My ears perked up when I heard they were interviewing a pastor. Pastor Craig Cooper was sitting on a stool, and sitting next to him was country music star Walker Hayes.

Together, they wrote a book called *Glad You're Here: Two Unlikely Friends Breaking Bread and Fences*. It was all about Walker's journey from atheist to Christian and Craig's patient, faithful, prayerful friendship that helped him get there. Craig didn't use a gospel tract that tried to literally scare the hell out of him. Instead, he just loved him.

Apparently, when they first met, Walker showed up to church still drunk from the night before. He only came out of a sense of obligation to his wife. Yet, Craig just shook his hand and said, "I'm glad you're here."[10] Hayes ended the *Good Morning America* segment by playing the song "Craig," which he wrote in honor of his friend. The first verse goes:

> I met Craig at a church called Redeeming Grace
> It's like he understood my "I don't wanna be here" face
> I felt out of place and I smelled like beer
> But he just shook my hand, said, "I'm glad you're here."[11]

After the segment ended, I found myself with tears in my eyes, thinking, *This is it. This is what evangelism looks like.* Friendship starts with meeting people where they are. Craig did just that. He didn't try to change Walker. He prayed for him, was there for him, and pointed to the one who could change him. That's what we're called to do.

We Start by Getting over Our Fear

What's stopping us from doing what Craig did? What's stopping us from genuine friendship as an incarnational bridge to Jesus? It's easy: fear. Fear of rejection. Fear of discomfort. Fear of being labeled. Even though that young couple handing a scare-the-hell-out-of-them card to me was misguided (in my opinion), at least they had the nerve to do it. Most Christians never risk that much. Hardly any of them risk anything at all.

According to *Lifeway Research*, "Half of Americans (51 percent) say they're curious as to why some people are so devoted to their faith, including 60 percent of the religiously unaffiliated."[12]

Basically, if you had ten random people in a room, five of them would be curious about your faith in Jesus (regardless of their own beliefs). Of course, it doesn't mean they would be interested in following Jesus (yet), but they would be game for conversations about Jesus. Those are pretty good odds.

But, as *Lifeway Research* also discovered, "74 percent of Christians have less than ten spiritual conversations a year."[13] In other words, a majority of Americans are open to having spiritual conversations, but only a small minority of Christians are willing to engage them. Those five in ten people would only see three in ten Christians respond. What is that saying about our willingness to share the *euangelion*?

Penn Jillette, the speaking half of the famous magic duo Penn & Teller, is an outspoken atheist. In early 2008, he had a vlog called *Penn Says*. In episode 192, he told the story of how a man gave him a Bible after a show and how impressed he was by the man's genuine concern for his soul. Although he is still an atheist, he said:

> I've always said that I don't respect people who don't proselytize. I don't respect that at all. If you believe that there's a heaven and a hell, and people could be going to hell or not getting eternal life, and you think that it's not really worth telling them this because it would make it socially awkward—and atheists who think people shouldn't proselytize and who say just leave me alone and keep your religion to yourself—how much do you have to hate somebody to not proselytize? How much do you have to hate somebody to believe everlasting life is possible and not tell them that? I mean, if I believed, beyond the shadow of a doubt, that a truck was coming at you, and you didn't believe that truck was bearing down on you, there is a certain point where I tackle you. And this is more important than that.[14]

What should we do about this? The church needs a kick in the pants. We need to risk to reach. We need to share the good news with gentleness and respect but also without fear.

We Must Create a Culture of Personal Invitation

How does your church fearlessly, gently, and graciously navigate this relational evangelism? The same way Craig did: through personal invitation that comes from genuine friendship. If you can create a culture of personal, incarnational invitation, you'll have the right posture for evangelism. Why? Because that's what loving people looks like. It's funny, with all the programming and community events, invitation that extends from personal relationship is still the undefeated champion of strategies. In a national survey conducted by *Lifeway Research*, "82 percent of the unchurched are at least 'somewhat likely' to attend church if they are invited."[15] And yet, most churchgoers don't invite. This is, in part, due to a lack of urgency or immediacy, but it's also due to a lack of practice. The key isn't just to invite. It's to create a church culture of personal invitation. Below are four tips for making it a part of the rhythm of your church.

Point, Invite, See

Since one of the big challenges of evangelism for congregation members is fear, how can we give them an easy-to-remember strategy to give them confidence? In John 1:35–39, we get a simple, repeatable model: point, invite, and see. After John the Baptist pointed to Jesus as "the Lamb of God," some of John's disciples decided to follow him. "Turning around, Jesus saw them following and asked, 'What do you want?' They said, 'Rabbi' (which means 'Teacher'), 'where are you staying?' 'Come,' he replied, 'and you will see.'"

Jesus's invitation to come and see feels more spiritual than literal. This is further emphasized when Andrew invites his brother, Simon, to come and see (in so many words) the Messiah. If we let our lives, in word and deed, point to Jesus, then, in love, we can invite people to discover Jesus themselves. Then, through the lens of faith, Jesus will help them see.

This approach can help your church members think through: *How do I share Jesus with my friends or family or fellow parents at the soccer fields?* Instead of hitting them over the head with gospel tracts or cleverly devised arguments, they can simply point and invite. Then, Jesus will help them see. As Jesus puts it in Matthew 5:16: "In the same way, let your light shine before others, that they may see your good deeds and glorify your Father in heaven." As we shine through genuine friendship/relationship, we are pointing to, and inviting them toward, Jesus.

Remove Barriers to Jesus

In Luke 15, we see the heart of the Father revealed. His desire is to seek and save the lost (for example, the lost coin, the lost sheep, and the lost son). As we saw in Chapter Five, the early church interpreted their inner conflict over Gentile inclusion by deciding to make it easier for them to turn to God. This posture has tons of practical applications.

You can ask, *How are we making it easier for seekers to find Jesus?* I'm not talking about seeker-sensitive services. I'm asking: How do we remove unnecessary barriers to Jesus? For example, your website is the front door of your church. This has been true for a long time, but especially since the pandemic. It's the portal through which people access worship streams, ministry information, and get-to-know-you before deciding to show up in person. You'd think the experience would be optimized for them, but it's often not. This is because insiders demand utility from your website (member directories, calendars, and committee information). But outsiders are looking for accessibility (relatable content, engagement opportunities, and overall feel).

Ask, *Is our web platform appealing? Is it easy to use? When a visitor engages, does anyone notice or follow up? Who is it for—the people we're trying to reach or the people we're trying to keep? If a visitor enjoys an online service, do they know what to do next?*

Of course, this isn't just for your online experience but for everything you do as a church. Is the way we do church making it easier or harder for people to come to know Jesus? This isn't about dumbing anything down—it's about dialing up understanding.

Make It Easy to Invite

Instead of a general come-to-church invite, give your congregation easy invitation opportunities. Maybe there's a fun Christmas event that isn't too churchy. Maybe there's a helpful parenting talk by a local expert. Maybe there's a pancake breakfast. Give churchgoers nonthreatening options. One-off events are perfect because they're a clear ask with clear, low-risk, high-value parameters. To make it even easier to invite, give your congregation easy ways to do it.

At Christmas, we make postcards that list all of our Christmas events and worship services. We encourage our members to take a stack of postcards and invite their friends. It's easier to hand someone a postcard and say, "I thought you might like to know about these wonderful Christmas opportunities" than a more general invitation to come to church. It's an easier way to make people who aren't naturally comfortable inviting invite others.

Unleash Excited People

Some of your best inviters will be the recently invited. Excitement happens when people feel that your church is changing their lives. When they're excited, they'll invite others to come along and experience it. It's kind of like when you find a new restaurant you like.

When we first started at Tower Hill, my wife and I found out about a little restaurant along the Navesink River (about five minutes from church). A few days a week in the summer, they have a two-for-one lobster special: two lobsters in big steaming pots with corn on the cob and potatoes, all for $31.95. Not only is the lobster amazing, but the whole vibe of the open-air picnic benches by the marina is delightful. We love this place so much that we always ask if newcomers have tried it yet. We bring family and friends. We invite because we're excited about it. We want others to experience what we love.

What's fascinating is that the longer someone has been at your church, the less likely they are to invite others. Why? Because their initial excitement has been tempered by familiarity. It doesn't mean they don't love the church. It just means that their fervor has changed into comfort. When that happens, the impulse to let everyone in on the restaurant (so to speak) has faded. Your newest church attenders are a powerful force. They are the most likely to invite others. But longtime members can be energized again, too. When they feel reawakened in their faith (which goes back to discipleship), they'll start inviting again. They'll want everyone to know about it.

Evangelism is the final gap before the next step in the process, which is generating your KRAs (key result areas) that will become the backbone of your plan. We'll discuss how to pick and prioritize these areas in the next chapter (and we'll begin the Decide phase of the 4D Process).

For Further Thought: Evangelism

- How can you cultivate relational evangelism with your congregation?
- What's an opportunity coming up where you can make it easy for your congregation to invite?
- What are the barriers that are preventing people from coming to Jesus?

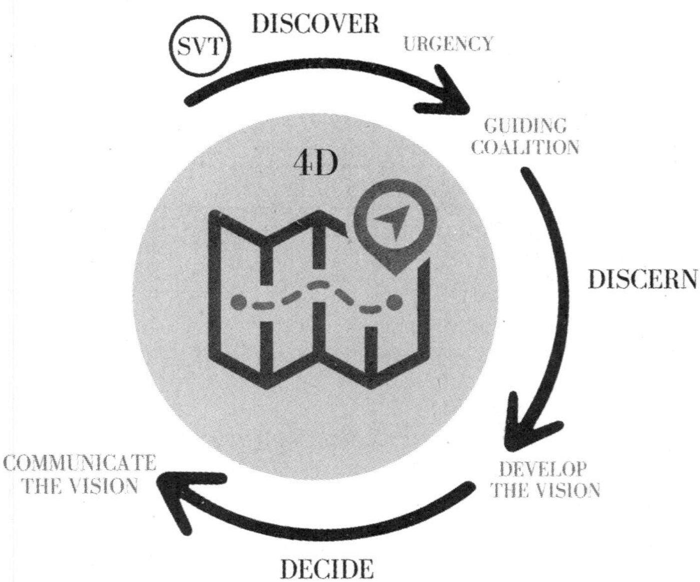

Chapter Nine

DEVELOPING KEY RESULT AREAS

A goal is not just about what you accomplish. It's about what you become.
—MICHAEL HYATT

In the Discern stage, we explored the art of gospel translation. We considered several gaps to address, based on the young families you're trying to reach: worship, next gen, discipleship, and evangelism. While there are certainly other gaps, these cover a lot of ground, enough to get an effective plan in place. Up until now, these chapters have been heavy on the *why* and more open-ended on the *what* as you've been discerning the vision. But at this point in the process, we flip it. We'll now get laser-focused on what, when, who, and how you're going to do it all.

Let me first acknowledge this: it's entirely possible that you've reached this point without doing anything in the Discover or Discern stage (yet). After all, you may want to get a sense of where this book is going before committing to the process. I get it. But just make sure you don't try to skip steps for the sake of speed. It won't work.

When I was twelve years old, my stepdad registered me to run a ten-kilometer race. I knew I was supposed to train, but I never really had the motivation. So I figured I would skip the long hours of jogging and just run the race. Not only did I barely finish, but it was a miserable experience, and I was sore for weeks. The 4D Process is designed to work step-by-step. Each part builds the endurance to run the race.

This is why consultants often don't work (and I am one). The expectation is that the consultant will magically parachute in and deliver a plan. Then it will save us all that jogging (the consultant will jog for us), and we can just run the race. They drop a beautiful plan in our laps with laminated, colorful pages full of graphs, charts, and core values. It's a plan that people look at and say: *See, we got something for our money.* But it typically doesn't work. Why? Because we didn't do the necessary work to understand, own, and fight for it. Training is the key to a successful race.

Once you've done the training and worked through the first two stages, it's time to run the race. If you're going to reach your God-given, God-driven ministry goals, you're going to need a good plan. It starts with deciding what key ministry areas you'll focus on to reach young families. We're now entering the Decide stage. It's at this point in the process that you'll finalize your vision and strategy and invite the rest of the congregation to help.

Leadership and the Dogsled

At this stage, you and your SVT are probably chomping at the bit to launch. After all, you've been talking about it for a while and have already been discussing viable translation methods (vision) to reach young families. Naturally, you'll always be the most excited and the most eager to get the ball rolling, and probably the least patient. That's typically a good sign (I mean, if you're not excited, who will be?). But it can also put a wrench in the works, because your instinct will be to run ahead faster (and farther) than the team is ready or willing to go. You'll need to lead from the front, alongside, and sometimes from behind—building consensus and collaboration along the way.

I learned this the hard way. In my first pastorate, right out of seminary, I rolled into town like Yosemite Sam from the old cartoons featuring Bugs Bunny—guns firing, with yells of "yee haw!" I knew what needed to be done, so I charged headlong into doing it. But in the end, I didn't build enough consensus and unity around the vision. In those three years, we made incredible change happen, including a new contemporary service that doubled our church attendance. But virtually all those changes disappeared the minute I left because they were almost entirely dependent on me. You don't need uniformity to make change stick—it's not that everyone needs to agree on everything. But you do need unity. You need different people with different gifts working together toward a shared vision.

It's kind of like driving a dogsled (an analogy I learned from Jesse Skiffington). Imagine that the ministry initiative or change you want to make is the cargo, and you'll use the sled to move it forward. You start by making sure the sled is the right size to carry the load. Do you know exactly what it's going to take to get it done? Have you counted the cost? Once you properly balance and secure the cargo, you can decide where to place the dogs (lead dogs out front, wheel dogs near the sled, team dogs in-between). Finally, you communicate clearly enough for the dogs to pull with energy, force, and efficiency.

But you can't just let them run full-out the whole time. You need to change speeds, depending on the terrain, or you can even apply the snow brake when necessary to maintain control. (I'm not suggesting your church team is composed of dogs, but you get the idea.) It's a balance between speed and security. It's this very balance you'll be straddling as you lead the process.

I don't know about you, but there's no way I would drive a dogsled without a lot of prayer. Prayer is the glue that keeps the sled and dogs together and ensures you don't get lost on the journey. Prayer must be supporting this entire process. In addition to your personal prayer, invite the SVT to pray with and for one another (without you). Make it a part of your regular meetings together. This will help develop their faith and trust in God because they are doing it, not just following you as you do it.

For the Discover stage and the Discern stage, you intentionally limited the 4D Process to your core leaders—your strategic vision team (SVT). This was critically important so you could do the deep work together: discovering who you are and who you're trying to reach and then discerning the necessary ministry gaps.

But now, in the Decide stage, it's time to open up and expand the conversation to the congregation. This is to ensure that they have a voice in the process. If they feel like they don't, they won't become co-owners of the vision. At some point, they'll stop pulling the sled. They'll just lie down in the snow, and you'll end up dragging them behind you (making everything much harder). Technically, this stage is where three of Kotter's steps come together. It's the final step in developing your strategic vision and the first big step in communicating that vision while enlisting a volunteer army to get it all done.

The Key Result Areas

A key result area (KRA) is simply an area that you will focus on to make successful gospel translation possible across generations. It's what you decide to *do* to address the meeting of needs you've *discerned*. For example, let's say you decide that adding a contemporary worship experience is going to be essential to reach young families. That's a KRA. Or maybe it's a desire to have more intergenerational fellowship. That's a KRA. It's the big idea, but it's not how you're going to accomplish the big idea. For example, with worship, you may decide on a Saturday night jazz service, a Wednesday evening prayer service, or something else. The KRA defines the what, but your ministry plan will determine the how. (We'll get to the plan in the Deploy stage.)

Remember, you're not starting with a blank slate. You already have an idea of the KRAs your church will need to address (worship service changes, Sunday school strategies, etc.) because of all the work you've done with the SVT. The SVT will be providing a report of their findings from stages one and two and will invite everyone else to weigh in on how to drive the dogsled forward. The best way to facilitate this is to invite your congregation to a KRA workshop.

The KRA Workshop

The best way I know to generate buy-in is to bring in. It's getting people in the same room to work it out, brainstorm, and discern together. It's kind of like getting your friends to go to Denny's at 2 a.m. (hypothetically). If it's just your idea and you drag your friends along, they'll complain the whole time. But if all of you decide to go, you'll enjoy every calorie of that Grand Slam. It changes everything if you decide together. You have to bring them into the decision-making process to get buy-in.

To bring in the congregation, you'll hold a one-day workshop at the church, where you'll have the SVT report their findings, decide on three to five KRAs, and form teams to start working on them. It's important that you invite all the key demographics in the church to join you. This is both a blanket and a targeted ask to get key stakeholders together—elders, deacons, key volunteers, staff, newcomers, and longtimers—with as much generational representation as possible. In other words, if there's anyone you want in the room, make sure they're invited. I would certainly make sure to include as many Gen Xers and millennials as possible to provide input on the young family strategies you'll discuss.

A word of encouragement: adding all these new voices will be incredibly valuable, but, don't be surprised if a few of them are absolutely insufferable. It's just how it works. Some people will say ridiculous things. *Maybe we should have a circus ministry because kids love the circus.* Or, *We should have a tambourine rack so people can grab one on their way into church.* While these aren't real suggestions, they elucidate a very real truth: not all feedback you get will be helpful. Some of it may be downright nasty. Not everyone will be on board for change, and that's normal (we'll talk more about that in Chapter Twelve). The important thing is to give them a place to vocalize their concerns.

But not all of the feedback is bad. You'll get some really good feedback, too. More often than not, it's in this stage that someone offers an insight that's absolutely critical. Again, if your SVT just told the congregation the plan, the congregation wouldn't adequately own the vision. You may be worried that you'll lose control of the vision by doing this; don't be. What you're concerned with at this stage isn't just about ideas but about recruiting the volunteer army necessary to put the ideas to work.

The structure for the KRA workshop should follow this general flow: develop urgency, report the work of the SVT, and invite the congregation to participate. As the KRAs emerge, congregation members will be invited to share their discussion insights, form task forces around each area, and commit to further action.

The Setup

Since this is a workshop and not a lecture, you'll want to gather around tables if possible. Due to the difficulty of getting this many people together, it's best to do it all at once (one day). For example, on a Saturday, start at nine o'clock in the morning and finish at two in the afternoon, with lunch in-between (see Figure 9.1 for a sample schedule). Sometimes, breaking it up into, let's say, a Friday night and a Saturday morning can work well—the danger is that you may lose people along the way.

Part One—Developing Urgency (30 Minutes)

This is where you share the *why* behind reaching young families. A great way to do this is to simply share the church decline data (both for the larger US church and your own congregation) from the Discover stage. The goal is for everyone in the room to feel the weight of inaction, to get them to step on the scale as you did. What is the opportunity cost if we do nothing or keep doing what we're currently doing?

What I've noticed about this strategy is that by sharing the data, it feels less like finger-pointing and tsk-tsking. It feels more objective instead of subjective. Instead of, Wow, they're saying we don't care about young people or we are failures, it's more like, Wow, younger generations see things very differently—that explains a lot. Hopefully, it compels them to consider what to do about it. Prior to the workshop, you may want to deliver a sermon (or a series) that builds a sense of urgency around the problem.

Part Two—Reporting the Work of the SVT (60 Minutes)

This is all about bringing the congregation up to speed on the analysis from the SVT so far and the process used to do it. The goal is to share who you are and who you're trying to reach (and the language barriers preventing you from doing it). Allow the SVT team (not you) to report on how they gathered information, put focus groups together, and what they learned about young families and the challenges the church has experienced in reaching them. Don't share the preliminary KRAs just yet. First, you'll want to hear from the people in the room (this is to foster a collaborative process instead of a prescriptive one). You're not telling them what you're going to do, but you are telling them who you're trying to reach (and why).

Part Three—Group Assessment (90–120 Minutes)

Get a few big pads of paper that you can put on easels (I like Post-it pads because you can hang the sheets easily). Then, ask people (at their tables) to discuss what they think the three greatest strengths of the church are (allow ten to twenty minutes). When they finish, invite each group to report their list for everyone to hear. As they do, write them down on one of the paper pads. Make connections between each group's assessment to show commonalities (I like to circle similar insights in different colors). Then, have the SVT report what their process revealed as the top three strengths of the church (about ten minutes). Make a point to highlight the agreement between the findings of the SVT and the group findings. This will build a sense of people deciding together.

Your ability to make connections based on what you're hearing in the room is like gospel translation, which is both an art and a science. It's pulling out ideas and saying, *I've heard us saying these three or four things*, or, *This is my take on what we've been saying; what do you think?* In other words, you're not a passive bystander. You're the master of ceremonies. You're an active participant as you synthesize the conversation in the room. This is why you don't have to worry about circus suggestions. You'll have some editorial control.

After you make the list of strengths, ask the groups to discuss what they think are the three greatest challenges of the church (again, ten to twenty minutes). (In a traditional SWOT analysis, we would say weaknesses, but this may sound too pejorative for some.) Then, follow the same process as making the list of strengths: invite each group to report, write them down on one of the paper pads, make connections, and have the SVT report their top three.

You may want to take a short break here, but you'll want to return quickly to decide what the final three to five KRAs are on your list (about thirty to sixty minutes). After discussing strengths and challenges and refining the KRAs, it's time to curate the list, to decide which items will be chosen, cut, added to, or adapted in a way that makes sense. Again, this is a role best filled by you. As the pastor and organizer, you will help bring clarity to the final list. As you go, you'll write the list of KRAs that will serve as the focal point for the remainder of the process. If you're nervous about this responsibility, have a couple members of the SVT do it with you. But don't hand this leadership opportunity away. It will galvanize trust. (Note: you'll likely have a few more KRAs that people are passionate about. That's fine: add them to a separate list.)

Most likely, there will be a great deal of consensus around the areas themselves; the challenge is trying to rank them in order of priority. Remember, whatever the group decides isn't binding. Your SVT can (and probably will) tweak the plan. What you're really looking for is agreement on the importance of your top two. So ask the group: *Out of the KRAs circled, what seems like the most important one to address first? Which ideas best utilize our strengths? What is the low-hanging fruit? What is the cost (emotional, financial)? What is the most urgent?* Then rank them accordingly.

Part Four—Build Teams around the KRAs (60 Minutes)

Post each individual KRA (using the paper pad) around the room. Then ask everyone to select the area they're most passionate about to engage in conversation. For example, if one KRA is a new worship style, another is a new Sunday school program, and another is launching small groups, each member will pick the area they most want to discuss. You'll now have three to five groups. Ask your SVT to split up between the different groups and lead the conversations around each KRA. Each group leader will simply ask: *What can we do to close the gap in this area?* A great way to start is with the suggestions that the SVT worked on prior to the workshop.

When you form the groups, you may have two people in one group and twenty-five in another. If that happens, simply do your best to even them out. Ask who can jump into another group. If you have a small church and you only have twenty people in the room, you may want to have each group handle multiple KRAs. Look for natural affiliations; the Sunday school program and small groups can be discussed together, for example. Then, you'll ask them to discuss: *What are some ideas to help us close the gap in this KRA? If we're going to reach young families, what are the things that we need to try to do to engage them? How do we speak their language? How do we understand their hopes and hurts? How do we know their dreams and pain points?* This is the brainstorming phase (and where you may hear about the circus). That's okay. Have the discussion leader write everything down.

Part Five—Sharing the Discussions (60 Minutes)

This will get you to the next step in developing your plan, and it's the end of the workshop. You'll invite each KRA group to share their insights (via a representative who will summarize their discussion). You'll invite the whole group to ask questions and get clarification. Then you'll do three things (and this is important). First, you'll thank everyone for participating in this process and how important they are to what God is doing in your church. Next, you'll ask if they'll commit to meeting with their group again to keep talking about how to achieve their KRA (within the next thirty days). Third, you'll make an important caveat. You'll tell them: *Our SVT will take all of this information and develop a draft for our strategic plan, and then they'll come back to you to brainstorm how to get it done.*

If you don't say this, the SVT will surrender control of the plan. You want to be clear up front that they are the curators and refiners of the action plan. By the way, most people will have no problem with this. But you've got to make sure that the expectation isn't *We do what the group suggests* but *We do what the leaders decide based on what the group suggests.*

After thirty days (or so), you'll have a representative from each KRA group join the SVT and share their further discussions. Then, the work of refining and final curating can begin. Your team will explore which ideas are viable, which ideas need some work, and which ideas need to be discarded. By the time you're done with this process, you'll have a list of KRAs and some ideas for how to accomplish them (but they are just ideas, not plans).

Turning the KRAs into a Plan

Now that you have a list, you still need to develop a plan. I feel like, at this point, I need to encourage you to take a breath and relax. This all feels like a lot. It is, but you're not doing this all at once. It happens over a couple months. Just because it's in the same step doesn't mean it has the same deadline. Now let's develop the plan.

There are typically five steps involved: evaluate existing programs, brainstorm new initiatives, analyze viability, determine low-hanging fruit, and decide the details (who, what, when, where, how). These are pretty straightforward, but let's unpack them a little.

First, you'll take a look at what you're already doing and ask: *Can any of these fulfill the purpose of the KRA, or can they be tweaked to work?* For example, we wanted to increase our reach to young families at Christmas. So we started by taking a look at our annual 'Round the Table Sing event. This beloved event started in the 1960s. It's what it sounds like—a carol sing-along event designed for young families. The problem was that, over the years, it had lost its effectiveness. There was waning enthusiasm from our musicians. Some were upset because the little kids weren't paying attention during the singing or seemed to just care about the cookies at the end. Others were downright red-faced about the kids acting like velociraptors when the cookies were served. Basically, it was a young family event perfectly designed for young families that were no longer in the room—those of previous generations.

But we already had some infrastructure around it. We had a prime spot carved out in the calendar for it. We still liked the idea of the event, and we started to imagine what it could look like if it were designed for this generation of young families. Ultimately, we ditched the tables and moved the event outside. Instead of a sit-down, it became a drop-in event based around an outdoor tree-lighting. We traded a sing-along for our band playing outside. We brought in firepits with s'mores, hot chocolate, and cookies. We added crafts for little kids. We had the kids choir come and sing right when the tree-lighting happened. We started offering photos with Santa. We used it to invite new young families to join us for Christmas Eve worship.

This reimagined event turned out to perfectly deliver on our KRA. But there are many current programs that can also work without needing such drastic tweaking. You may (and probably do) have programs that are just a small adjustment away from accomplishing exactly what you need. So take a good look at them before brainstorming new ones, which is the second step.

Brainstorming is my favorite part. Surround me with whiteboards and coffee, and I'm happy. But one of the myths about brainstorming is that you're always pulling ideas out of thin air. For most churches, this isn't a strength. One of the biggest challenges for longtime members is a lack of imagination (it's hard for them to visualize a different way of doing things). So how can we get them to brainstorm new initiatives? You get the ideas from somewhere else.

The brainstorming process that will give you the greatest chance of success is more about collecting ideas. Read books together as a team, reach out to other churches (take a field trip and see what they do that works), attend conferences together, have coffee with other pastors, listen to podcasts (I know a great one), collect ideas. Then, when you find something you like, ask: *How do we translate what they do into our context?*

The third step is to analyze the viability of the idea. *Do we have the resources to do this? If not, what do we need? What are the real obstacles in our way? Are those obstacles internal (within our control) or external (outside our control)? What are the expectations of our current and future members? What needs to happen if we are to do this successfully?* By asking these questions, you can determine whether or not to keep moving forward or if you need to readjust.

Then, once you land on an idea, it's time to ask: *How can we get some quick wins as we move this ministry initiative forward? What is the low-hanging fruit?* If you can get some quick wins, it will generate enormous excitement (and even more buy-in) because it will show a proof of concept. Your congregation will start to believe. For example, we had a KRA to develop small group ministries from scratch. Our church was completely unfamiliar with this model, so we decided to offer a tasty sample: our version of "dinners for eight" (a popular model of fellowship for many churches).

This is where you invite people to sign up, and you place them in a dinner group that will meet in people's homes or at the church over a period of time (typically once a month for three to four months). Ours had a twist. We knew our folks loved going out to eat more than going to someone's house. So we made reservations at local restaurants. When the participants got there, they were told where they were going (and who they were matched up with). It was a one-off event, just trying to show the impact of being together in a small group. We had group leaders bring a few icebreaker questions with them to facilitate conversation. Our people loved it. It was a quick, easy win. We didn't have our small groups planned out yet. We didn't have the leaders trained. But we were able to do something to generate excitement right away.

What If We Could?

At this point, you have a strategic vision and a draft of a plan. In the next chapter, we'll start to finalize that plan and roll it out. But before we do, I want to address something that will probably happen a few times during the Decide stage. You'll have people in the congregation and even some in your inner circle who hear an idea and say: *We could never do that.* They'll cite your lack of resources or your history (*We tried that years ago, and it didn't work*). They'll try to tone down the ideas so they're more palatable. Sometimes, they'll argue that you (the church) really just need to do what you're already doing—just better. But if what you were doing was already working, you wouldn't need this process, would you?

A strategy that I love to use is to ask: What if we could? To be honest, I can't remember if I came up with this question or if I learned it from Andy Stanley. As you've no doubt noticed, he's been a pretty big influence on me. Here's how it works: When you're challenged with those who think something's impossible, simply ask, *What if we could?*

Pastor, we can't do that, they say.

You're right, I say. *We probably can't, but what if we could?*

Well, then you'd have to do this, or, *We'd need to think about this*. When you ask *What if we could?*, it gets them thinking about what it would take to do it. In a way, they go into problem-solving mode instead of just naysayer-mode. It works because it's an invitation to imagine, to trust, and to leave no stone unturned when trying to be faithful to God's mission.

Figure 9.1. Sample Schedule KRA Workshop

8:45 a.m. Welcome	Coffee, light fare
8:55 a.m. Open with Prayer	
9:00 a.m. Developing Urgency	Share the discover-stage research and help attendees see the urgency of the problem.
9:30 a.m. SVT Report	Let the SVT share their process and discoveries about the problem and initial ideas.
10:30 a.m.	Break
10:45 a.m. Group Assessment	The table groups will brainstorm possible KRAs in light of the information. The goal is 3–5 KRAs.
12:30 p.m.	Lunch
1:30 p.m. KRA Teams	Once KRAs are set, invite the congregation to pick one where they will discuss possible initiatives.
2:30 p.m. KRA Team Reports	Have each team report their discussion and conclusions. Leave time for Q&A.
3:30 p.m. Close with Prayer	

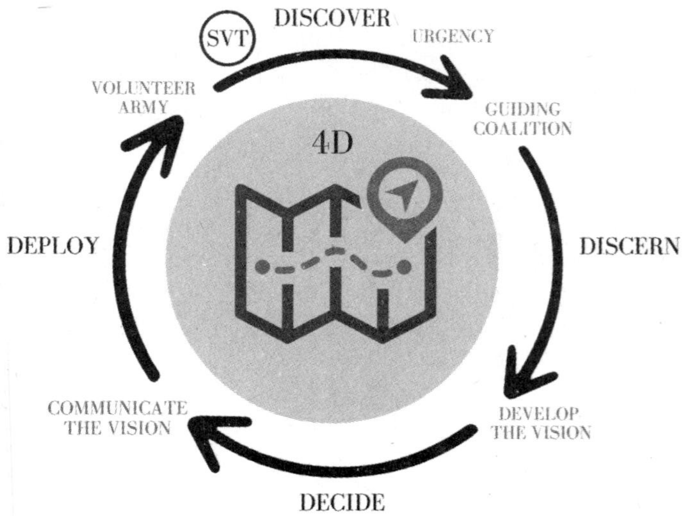
SVT
DISCOVER
URGENCY
GUIDING COALITION
DISCERN
DEVELOP THE VISION
DECIDE
COMMUNICATE THE VISION
DEPLOY
VOLUNTEER ARMY
4D

Chapter Ten

DEFYING GRAVITY

A goal without a plan is just a wish.
—ANTOINE DE SAINT-EXUPÉRY

On October 14, 2024, SpaceX successfully launched, then landed, its *Starship* rocket, "a fully reusable transportation system designed to carry both crew and cargo to Earth orbit, the Moon, Mars and beyond."[1] The booster rocket, known as Super Heavy, was "the most powerful launch vehicle ever developed,"[2] weighing in at a staggering eight million pounds. It could carry one hundred fifty tons of payload. The amount of thrust needed to launch *Starship* is pretty mind-blowing: "Its thirty-three raptor engines generate sixteen million pounds of thrust."[3]

I was a pretty mediocre physics student in high school, but I do remember my teacher explaining how space launches work. All the heavy lifting (so to speak) happens the closer you are to the surface of the Earth. It takes tremendous energy just to get an inch off the ground. But as the vehicle travels higher and the air gets thinner, it takes less and less force to break through the atmosphere. Once you're in orbit, you do virtually no work to stay there—just utilizing small, strategic thrusts to put the spacecraft in the desired orientation.

This is exactly like launching your plan. As you may have noticed, the first three stages of the translation process—discover, discern, and decide—take a lot more time and energy. Now is when we start getting into thinner air and letting momentum carry us higher. It's time to put that hard work into action in the Deploy stage. At this point, while the gravitational pull of status quo still takes work to overcome, the fuel burn of the initial stages (and the calculations it took to push through them) will hurl you forward.

Status Quo Bias

Launching is all about fighting the relentless pull of gravity. For churches, that gravitational pull is the status quo. It seems like every time we introduce change, it always wants to snap back, like a rubber band, to how things were before. Some of that is a systems issue (which we'll discuss in the next chapter). Regardless, it's almost always because of the sheer force of status quo, which is constantly threatening to pull us back to the ground and which takes a lot of energy to overcome.

Have you ever wondered why? Apparently, status quo is kind of like a human brain default setting. It's called status quo bias, and it influences almost every decision we make. "This bias is so deeply ingrained in our psyche that it often operates below our conscious awareness, silently steering us toward the familiar and away from change."[4] Have you ever wondered why, when you enjoy a particular meal at a restaurant, you tend to order it over and over again? Status quo bias. Or why you want to go back to the same vacation spots year after year? Status quo bias. Or why you enjoy the same morning routine before work? Or why your grandmother still rocks a beehive hairdo? Bad taste. Just kidding. Status quo bias. It's our deeply embedded desire to do the familiar over the unfamiliar.

There's comfort in the familiar, in the known. But this can also hurt us, because the known isn't always the good or the right thing. We'll repeat activities, patterns, and processes that are painful or even harmful because we want to avoid the unknown. It's like that idiom: "Better the devil you know than the devil you don't." Personally, I'd like to steer away from all devils.

That's why change is so hard to get an inch off the ground. It's decidedly uncomfortable (even good change), because it's going somewhere unfamiliar. For churches, this can be (and often is) crippling—it prevents us from fulfilling our purpose, the Great Commission. In fact, it leads to something of a great omission: the decision (consciously or unconsciously) to exclude those who aren't already a part of the community. Status quo turns us inward instead of outward. We start caring more about member satisfaction than outsider interaction. This stops gospel translation from ever taking off.

We Must Remember Who We Are

I once heard Simon Sinek, a thought leader in the business world, make a marketplace analogy that I'll apply to the church. You don't buy a car because you want to buy gasoline. The gas is a critical part of operation of the car—it helps get you where you want to go—but it's not why you buy the car. You buy the car because of where you want it to take you. In church life, the gas is the membership, the people who make the engine of ministry run. But the engine doesn't exist for its own sake; it exists to move the car to its destination, the world to which God sends us. That's precisely why many churches struggle to get anywhere—they're acting like they bought the car for the gas.

Christ's church is a Word–flesh reality. It's both supernatural and sociological (institutional). On one hand, the church is an event. Through faith in Jesus Christ, we are supernaturally ingrafted, adopted, chosen, made alive, recreated, and reconciled—we "who were once far away [are] brought near by the blood of Christ" (Eph. 2:13). Yet, the church is also the coordination and organization of people, with systems and standards and styles that reflect their shared life together. It's both a movement of God and an institution of people. The institution in itself isn't the problem. The problem is when institutional needs are elevated over the needs of the movement.

When the institution becomes the primary activity of the church, most energy is spent on maintenance instead of mission. This reduces the thunder and fire of translation into nothing more than a program to manage. We essentially ignore the purpose to which we've been called. The church isn't just a gathering of like-minded religious individuals who voluntarily decide to exist based on shared beliefs and interests. We are the *ekklesia*, the called-out ones, created by God, by the movement of the Holy Spirit. God calls out (1 Pet. 2:9), gathers (Eph. 2:13), equips (Eph. 4:12), and sends (Matt. 28:19–20) the community of faith into the world to share the good news of the in-breaking of the kingdom of God in Christ Jesus.

In the first quarter of 2008, Starbucks had its "worst three-month performance in its history as a public company.[5] Managers cited the economy and competition as the culprits. Howard Schultz (the newly returned CEO) told the company that the real problem was that they'd forgotten their mission: "even more than perfecting our coffee, we had to restore the passion and the commitment . . . for our customers."[6] What Schultz knew, is that when you forget your mission, you forget your purpose. And, when that happens, it becomes nearly impossible to move forward effectively.

Unless the church remembers its mission, we won't be able to effectively translate. We become lost in translation, as does God's good news to the world. We need to remember our purpose: the *Missio Dei*. We need to remember who we are and why God calls and sends us. It's like *The Lion King*. When Simba is driven into the jungle by fear, he starts to forget who he is. Instead of saving the pride lands (his purpose), he hangs out with Timon and Pumbaa while the hyenas run amok. He becomes lost. Then, he hears his father's spirit exhort him: "Remember who you are." Likewise, I can hear our heavenly Father exhorting us to do the same. We exist for the sake of God's mission to the world. We need to get out of the jungle and face the challenges ahead.

It Takes Discipleship and Strategic Action

Why talk about God's mission and our purpose at this point in the process? Because to successfully deploy, you'll need to help frame it for your congregation in a way that gives them kingdom of God perspective. They'll need the why right in front of them or else they'll be quick to snap back to status quo. It's here that we must lift up the most underrated and oft-ignored aspects of leading church revitalization: the spiritual growth of the congregation as you execute the plan.

It's been my experience that change begins in the hearts of the people and extends to the strategic plan. As Reggie McNeal puts it in *A Work of Heart*:

> What we see on the American religious landscape are scores of institutionalized expressions of Christianity that lack spiritual vibrancy or a sense of mission that moves beyond mere survival needs. These congregations frenetically search for new ways to "do church" or to accomplish their vision without attending to the fundamental heart issues of their constituency. No methodological fix can stir these groups into being spiritually prepared to practice an obedience that will bring them into an active partnership with God in his mission in the world.[7]

We're not just looking for best practices or new and shinier ways to do church. Our revitalization efforts are a byproduct of discipleship. This is how we elevate movement over institution. As we draw near to God, we embrace God's mission and rely on the Spirit's power to declare the wonders of God in the language of the people.

If your church is to fulfill its gospel-mandated mission, it must begin with the decision to turn to God (individually and communally). It is precisely in this turning that a kind of spiritual heart surgery occurs; the sinner's heart is shaped by and reflects more and more the heart of God. When this happens, you remember who you are and what you need to do. As you prepare to roll out your plan, you'll notice a kind of two-pronged approach that tends to both the KRAs and the overall discipleship of the congregation.

Prioritizing the KRAs

At this point, you should have your list of KRAs and what you've decided to do. Now it's time to prioritize and execute the plan—specifying the when, the who, and the how. This is an area where churches often get stuck. What can happen is that churches can end up going backward to the Decide or even Discern stage because they feel they need more data. I once worked at a church that had the exact same conversation about the location of a dumpster in the parking lot for three years. The reason? The committee working on it was being led by the process thinker of all process thinkers. They never had "enough information" to move forward. (As an aside, I don't know if it was ever moved.)

Of course, poring over the data is critical, but indecision is most often a stall tactic. There is no reason a church can't make a big, strategic decision within ninety days. Yet, anxiety over change can bring everything to a screeching halt. The way I approach this is to explain and ask: *You'll never have all the information available, but do you have enough information to make an educated decision?* The clock is ticking. Our high schoolers are about to graduate. Our preschoolers are jumping to kindergarten. Our young families are making decisions about what matters most in their schedules. It's time to get started.

A way to help alleviate their concern is to remind them that launching the ministry initiatives for each KRA doesn't have to happen all at once. Chances are you don't have all the resources (human or financial) needed anyway. So you can work in stages. This is a good thing because it helps protect the integrity of the process. For example, if you launch everything at once, you'll instantly drive a competition for resources, and many of the same people will be working on multiple initiatives (thus increasing the chance of burnout). Taking things one project at a time helps you launch together and can buy time to keep processing in other areas if needed.

It's time to prioritize the work. Using the simple chart shown at Figure 10.1, you're going to rank your KRA plans according to four factors: urgency, impact, complexity, and cost. Let's quickly unpack each category.

Urgency is an important factor to name. In the church world (and I suppose in the rest of the world), every challenge feels urgent and immediate. But not all of them are. Ask, *If we don't address this ministry area soon, will it break irreparably?* Or, *Can it wait while we figure out some other areas?* Label each KRA plan according to urgency (one to five), one being lowest and five being highest.

Next, consider the potential impact. *Which ministry area is creating the biggest obstacle to our church health? How could addressing a particular area create a domino effect in other areas?* Sometimes this has to do with understanding what moves the needle for people to act. For example, two years ago, we needed a capital campaign. It consisted of two buckets: facility projects (painting, carpeting, tarring the parking lot) and new, upgraded ministry spaces for our teenagers (more breakout and hangout rooms). Guess which bucket had the most energy around it? It was the excitement and energy around reaching young people with the gospel that had a huge impact on getting everything else done. Label each KRA plan according to impact (one to five).

Now, think about complexity. You may believe that renovating the sanctuary is the most urgent and impactful plan to chase. But is it too complex to realistically tackle first? Will it put too much of a delay on all the other critical ministry plans? Will it be a tailwind or a headwind in your launch? This is important to consider. Ask, *What are the obstacles (internal or external) that must be overcome (expectations of members, lack of resources, etc.)?* And, *How much organizational energy will it take to overcome these obstacles?* Label each according to complexity (one to five).

Finally, you'll consider cost. Financial cost is of course a primary factor. When assessing this, make sure you have the most accurate estimates and proposals available, and then build in an extra 10–20 percent for overages (we'll talk more about funding in the next chapter). It's not just a financial determination—you'll need to consider the opportunity cost of doing nothing. *What is the potential benefit our church will forfeit by failing to act? How much worse, or unhealthy, will our congregation become? How much further will we be from translating the gospel to young families in our community?* Label each according to cost (one to five).

Once the table is filled, simply total the numbers and rank each KRA plan from highest to lowest, between a maximum of twenty and a minimum of four. This will give you the order in which to create strategic action around each plan. Now it's time to put everything together for successful deployment: prioritized strategic action and discipleship.

Assembling Your Strategic Plan

There's a memorable scene from *Apollo 13* in which the team back on Earth has to find a way to scrub the carbon dioxide from the lunar module before the astronauts run out of breathable air. The camera focuses on an engineer bursting into the room, dumping a bunch of spare parts on a table, and saying, "We've got to find a way to make this fit into the hole for this, using nothing but that." To this day, it's one of my favorite examples of the kind of strategic thinking necessary for churches to move change forward. It takes urgency, creativity, adaptability, and utility.

Typically, we don't have the time or the money to just buy our way out of problems. We have to be scrappy. We have to make use of what we have to do what needs to be done. We have to think our way out. Strategy is about closing the gap between where you are and where you want to go by using what you have at your disposal.

For example, at Tower Hill, our big KRA was moving the contemporary service from the fellowship hall to the sanctuary on Sunday mornings. We had outgrown the space, and after a lot of study and discussion, we agreed that the move was necessary. But we had some challenging parameters. The first was that whatever we did, we couldn't disrupt the traditional environment. The goal was for contemporary elements to be invisible (at least mostly) to the traditional worshipers. At the same time, we also knew that we needed to overcome and completely transform the traditional environment for the contemporary service. We only had thirty minutes between services to do it. No easy task.

How did we do it? We got scrappy. We bought some new gear, but we also repurposed gear from around the church. We discovered that the biggest bang for our buck was to use LED lighting to change the environment. Our property manager was a skilled carpenter, and he found ways to hide things like motorized window shades and confidence monitors. We used what we had as best we could.

But we still didn't know how to overcome the time. This was a problem until I attended the Drive Conference at North Point Community Church. It was the first session, and Andy Stanley was speaking. After he closed us in prayer, the stage went dark and a video played. Thirty seconds later, the lights came back on, and a nine-piece worship band had magically taken Andy's place on stage. *That's it!* I thought to myself. *If they can do it in thirty seconds, we can do it in thirty minutes. We can make all the traditional furniture moveable—put it on wheels. We can use wireless mics and instrument packs to speed up the transition time (no taped-down cables).*[8] I drew a picture of it in my notebook (pictured below at Figure 10.2).

The next step was to plan what we needed to do to see it through. We had to close the gap. It's now time for you to do the same. Based on all the work you've done so far, let's finalize the strategic plan: formation, implementation, and communication.

Final Plan Formation

By now, most of your strategy formation is probably set. That is, you've decided what you're going to do and have at least a rough sense of who will do it and how it'll get done. The Spirit is in the details. Let's get a bit more granular to break down your KRA initiative into actionable steps.

How do you eat an elephant? One bite at a time. What are the bites you'll need to take to complete the plan? It's like planning a trip. A couple of years ago, my wife and I were invited to Grand Cayman for a wedding. We didn't just wake up one morning and decide: *Hey, let's jump on a plane and go to the Cayman Islands.* It took a couple months of preparation—getting passports, securing hotel and rental car reservations, and deciding which sightseeing opportunities we would try and cram into our short visit. What's the itinerary for your ministry trip? What will be first, second, third, etc.? How long will it take? How will you know when it's time for the next step? Who is responsible for what?

You're probably familiar with the idea of SMART goals (specific, measurable, achievable, relevant, and time-bound). Or maybe you've heard of FAST goals (frequently discussed, ambitious, specific, and transparent). Or, maybe you want SMART and FAST. You may find both of these helpful (see Figure 10.3) as you break your plan down into actionable steps.

By the time it's done, everyone on the team should know the expectations of who, what, when, where, and how the plan will move forward. Perhaps the most important aspect is that they'll help you determine a reasonable time frame for each action item (with deadlines). You can always change a deadline, but if you never have one, everything will take you longer, and you'll miss out on the unity created by working together toward a focused goal.

Maybe you're wondering who is going to do it? You have the leadership to help (SVT), but this is where you'll officially invite the KRA idea teams to become KRA implementation teams. After you develop the strategic plan, you'll send it to the teams and assign tasks for them to carry out. They are going to be the first wave of the volunteer army you'll use to make the change happen.

Plan Implementation

This is where you put what's on paper into real life. Perhaps it's no surprise, but many churches never get this far. Not because the work is too hard, but because doing the thing is a lot scarier than endlessly talking about the thing. I came across an article by Lon Roberts, who talked about a situation during World War II, when Winston Churchill heard that:

> the designers of the landing craft that would transport tanks and troops across the Channel were spending the bulk of their time debating major design changes, [and] he issued this warning: The maxim "Nothing avails but perfection" may be spelt shorter: "Paralysis."[9]

Sometimes this is referred to as analysis paralysis, but I agree with Churchill that it's more of a kind of perfection paralysis. Implementation is all about overcoming your fear of perfection. There's a fine line between getting your ducks in a row and tying yourself in knots through perfectionism. This is what gets you stuck and causes you to lose the battle (so to speak).

In 2015, I heard Guy Kawasaki speak at the Catalyst conference in Atlanta. He helped Apple sell the Macintosh in the 1980s, and he had a great take on maintaining a healthy perspective during implementation: *just ship it.* When launching new computer products (hardware, software), he explained how the tyranny of perfection would often bring progress to a grinding halt. "Don't try to achieve perfection," he said. "Sometimes you just have to ship it. You can always release a 2.0 version next year."

I think that's great advice. You've done the work. You've put the plan together. Now, ship it. It won't be perfect, but you don't need perfection to be faithful (just look at the disciples). Popular speaker and author Jon Acuff (at the same conference) said that the key to implementing change is to "be a tourist." Why? Because tourists have a sense of wonder. They have a joy about their meandering and aren't embarrassed to ask for directions.

That trip to Grand Cayman took a lot of planning, and planning always comes with anxiety. *Do we have to pay a fee for our cell phones to work? What if we miss our connecting flight? What if they lose our luggage? What if we crash driving on the other side of the road?* (We didn't crash, by the way, but there were moments.) There were always unknowns. But it didn't stop us. When we got there, we went full tourist. We had so much fun. We swam in the ocean, ate rum cake, and held sea turtles.

Make detailed plans, but also hold them loosely. Stay flexible and adaptable. Be a tourist, not a perfectionist. Hold on and enjoy the trip. It'll be full of beauty, and yes, some anxiety over the unknown. I'll put it to you plainly: something will go wrong. But so much will go right. It's not all out of your control, however. A huge piece to ensuring smoother travel and mitigating risk is to make sure you are communicating every step of the way.

Plan Communication

We've spent almost ten chapters talking about how to translate the gospel for young families. But that's not the only translative work we're doing. We need to effectively translate the mission, vision, KRAs, and the plan(s) in such a way that the people want to join in. We need to generate buy-in. This is where you'll think in terms of a two-pronged approach (strategy and discipleship) to communicate the strategic vision with the congregation.

Let's say our KRA is to overhaul our Sunday school to increase our reach and impact on the next gen. It'll require some financial and relational investment to renovate some classrooms, select new curriculum, and recruit more volunteers. How do you start communicating it? TPGWGDTRC, of course. The acronym just rolls off the tongue, right? Okay, maybe not. But it works.

Theme It

Give a theological and scriptural anchor to it. Perhaps Nehemiah could be a solid foundation, with the image of families standing in the gaps to fight for Jerusalem. Perhaps a call to action would be to stand in the gap to help the next generation. Giving it a theme, or naming it, makes it portable, memorable, and focused. This will help unify the message and build shared language around it.

Preach It

Then, unpack it in a sermon series. Perhaps you will go through Nehemiah over six weeks. As you do, you will share what you discovered, discerned, and decided, simultaneously building a sense of urgency by sharing the data and laying out the *Missio Dei.* A call to action could be to join one of the KRA teams in their implementation work.

Go Wider with It

As you're talking about it in the sermon series, you'll give the congregation a chance to join the conversation. Hold one or two town-hall style meetings composed of two parts: a presentation (where you'll, again, unpack the why, what, and how) and a question-and-answer session with the SVT and Leadership Team (LT). (Tip: have members of the team field as many questions as possible to show it's not just the pastor's ideas.)

Go Deeper with It

Again, during the six weeks, have at least one group of five to twelve people discuss it, pray for it, and go deeper with the Scripture around it. A small group Bible study is a perfect way to do this. If you have small groups, have them all do it during the sermon series. If you don't have small groups, this could be the perfect opportunity to start one (or more). Invite people to discuss how to stand in the gap. Invite them to volunteer one week for Sunday school—get them to join the mission as they absorb the mission.

Triage It

Connect with dissenters or detractors early and often. Don't wait—if one person who has any influence is upset, it will spread like wildfire throughout the congregation. What I've discovered is that, usually, they are upset over miscommunication. Seek them out (don't wait for them to come to you). Have your ear to the ground on this—ask small group leaders to let you know about them, etc. Then approach them with something like, *Hey, I heard you're not happy with our plans—I want to make sure we do it right, so I'd love to hear your feedback.* Then listen. They may have valid concerns that, if you address them, may make all the difference in successful implementation. (We'll talk about this more in the next chapter.)

Repeat It

After your sermon series, create another touchpoint for the congregation. My favorite way is to record a quick, unpolished video on my phone (about three minutes) that takes some of the data, theological ideas, and call(s) to action and pulls them together. For example, a quick video about giving/volunteering for Sunday school. Yes, you can use an email instead of video, but video will always be more compelling. The idea is that you send this out to your email list to reinforce your sermon series, reach those who missed it, or help create a call to action, a next step for people to take.

Celebrate It

Last, but not least, celebrate the wins. What's a win? Any forward movement. Talk about it, clap for it, and share it with joy. *We raised half our money needed! We welcomed two new families! We're becoming the kind of church that stands in the gap for the next generation!*

If you're going to get more than an inch off the ground, you'll need the thrust force of gospel unity, which, according to Ephesians, is how we "become mature, attaining to the whole measure of the fullness of Christ" (Eph. 4:13). It's everyone working together for the sake of the mission.

Figure 10.1. Prioritizing KRAs

Urgency	Impact
Complexity	Cost

Figure 10.2. Journal Drawing

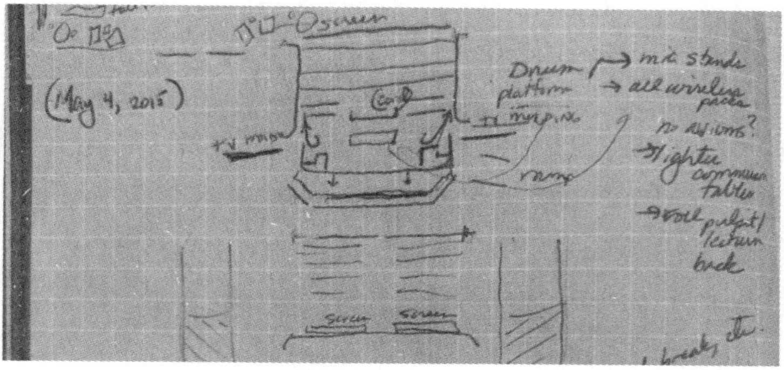

Figure 10.3. SMART and FAST Goals

Specific	Is it clear what the goal is?
Measurable	By what metrics will it be evaluated?
Achievable	Is it realistic according to the time and resources available?
Relevant	Does it make sense according to the overall vision?
Time-Bound	What is the specific timeline?
Frequently Discussed	How can you make it part of your regular communication?
Ambitious	Is it big enough to inspire action?
Transparent	Is it hidden from people or in plain view?

Chapter Eleven

THE THINGS THAT GO BOOM

Discipline, not the Muse, results in productivity. If you write only when she beckons, your writing is not yours at all.
—KENNETH ATCHITY

The mission on the wall is only as good as the system down the hall.
—ANDY STANLEY

Thirty years ago, I spent a summer working at a wilderness camp near the Boundary Waters in Minnesota. I do mean wilderness camp. We had no electricity or running water. We ground our own wheat and used a basic outhouse—a shack with a hole in the ground. We slept in individual, two-man tents in the middle of the forest, and we had to build fires if we wanted hot water. I can't imagine doing that for even twenty-four hours now, but I was young back then, and I was supremely confident in my ability to adapt to wilderness life.

One night, as we finished a group campfire and were getting ready to turn in, I realized I'd forgotten my flashlight. It was about a five-minute walk to my tent, so I didn't think much of it. When my friends realized it, they offered to walk me to my tent. For some reason—call it hubris or arrogance, or the fact I was trying to impress everyone—I declined and said something like: *I can see enough in the dark to follow the trail.*

Except, I couldn't. I realized it too late. Once everyone else left the fire and headed to their tents, I found myself alone on the darkest trail I've ever been on. I tried to feel the trail with my feet.

It kind of worked, as I shuffled along slowly, but I kept ending up in the bushes. I thought about yelling for help at one point but just couldn't bring myself to that level of shame. Eventually, I got on my knees so I could feel the trail with my hands. My watch had an electroluminescent backlight on it that emitted a bright, blue-green light. I pressed the button every few minutes and held it close the ground so I could see about four inches of trail at a time. That's how I got to my tent—on my hands and knees, four inches at a time. Guess how long that five-minute walk took? About an hour and half.

It's easy to get lost, or off mission, when launching change. There are times you'll need to ask for help, let someone share their light, and not feel like you have to do everything alone. If you don't, at best, you'll inch along to your destination. At worst, you may experience a failure to launch. The point is that execution is a team sport. In this part of the Deploy stage, you'll need to mobilize your congregation. So how do you make sure your launch is as effective and efficient as possible? Discipline.

The Art of Discipline

I used to think the creative writing process was primarily about inspiration. What I've discovered is that it's mostly about perspiration. While inspiration certainly plays a role, there are days when it's just not there. But there are deadlines to keep and "miles to go before I sleep."[1] The real key is discipline—sitting in front of the screen or notebook and putting pen to paper (or fingers to keyboard). It's setting word-count goals, even if the words are clunky. Somerset Maugham, an English writer, was asked about the role of inspiration. "I write only when inspiration strikes," he replied. "Fortunately, it strikes every morning at nine o'clock sharp."[2]

Deployment is about execution. Execution is about discipline. There are days you're going to wake up and not want to show up. That's perfectly normal. However, the difference between a successful launch and an unsuccessful launch is about the consistency of execution over time—finding the discipline to act every single day. The best way to do that is to bake it into what you're already doing.

I always tell my congregation that the secret to discipleship isn't to rearrange your daily routine but to find a way to leverage your routine to be more present to God. By inserting intentional prayers and practices into mundane rhythms, you can be more connected with God. I believe KRA execution works in a similar way. You were already busy before you decided to lead change. You were already working all your hours. The answer isn't to change everything about how you spend your precious time—it's to leverage the time you're already spending.

In 2016, I came across a book at an Atlanta airport bookstore: *The 4 Disciplines of Execution*. The book helped give me a framework to better execute change. Once I understood each discipline, I figured out how to incorporate them into what I was already doing to successfully launch. Let's go through each one, and I'll show you what I mean.

The Four Disciplines

The first discipline is to focus on "your wildly important goal."[3] This is about remembering your *why*. One of the most important roles you'll have is to not only create, but maintain, a sense of urgency about the ministry goal. Goal execution takes time. Over time, people lose their steam and excitement for the work. But if you keep it in front of them, you'll infuse new energy. Talk about or pray about your goal at every meeting, worship service, and Bible study. Tell stories of progress, and celebrate the forward movement. If you can keep the why in front of them, it will be the guiding star that keeps them driving the what.

The second is to "act on lead measures."[4] This one may not be quite as intuitive. When evaluating performance, there are lag indicators and lead indicators. Lag indicators tell you where you've been. These were the indicators you used, for example, in the Discover and Discern stages. They paint a picture of your past and current state. But to get forward movement, you need to focus on lead indicators. They predict future outcomes. They are the pieces that will help fill in the puzzle picture of the church you hope to be as a result of the KRAs. It's another way of saying: *focus on the solution*. Instead of a lag indicator of Sunday school attendance, focus on a lead indicator of new families signing their kids up. *How do we increase engagement? How do we find a curriculum or approach that will excite both kids and parents? How do we make the Sunday school experience so compelling that it draws them in?* If you focus on lead measures, it will keep your plan moving forward.

The third discipline is to "keep a compelling scoreboard."[5] This is just what it sounds like. Think of a giant thermometer often displayed to show fundraising progress. It's almost gamifying the goal. That's why I'm big on themes and vision boards. If your goal is discipleship, count the baptisms and small group growth, giving and engagement. Show how it all tells a story of spiritual growth.

The final discipline is to "create a cadence of accountability."[6] If there are no deadlines or deliverables, how will you measure your distance to the finish line? It's like a college term paper. The only reason it gets done is because the professor holds your feet to the fire and checks in on your progress along the way. Developing a cadence means baking it into your process. This often looks like a weekly (or regular) meeting where the key leaders review the scoreboard. *How much forward movement are we getting? Where are we in filling the thermometer? What actions do we need to focus on this week?* These are questions that I simply add to our standing leadership meetings.

The Two Big Failure Points

No matter how well-planned your launch or how many of the four disciplines you utilize, there can still be catastrophic failure. For example, despite NASA's diligent safety and systems checks, an oxygen tank still exploded two days into the Apollo 13 mission in 1970. "After the accident, NASA quickly established the Apollo 13 Review Board."[7] NASA spent two months investigating why the explosion occurred (and who was to blame). The board discovered that it was most likely "an electrically initiated fire in oxygen tank No. 2 in the service module."[8] This fire, they believed, "resulted from an unusual combination of mistakes, coupled with a somewhat deficient and unforgiving design."[9] In other words, it was both a human failure and a design or system failure.

Your ministry launch can face both challenges as well. If you're going to maintain acceleration until you're up and out of the atmosphere, it's important to understand some of the malfunctions that can happen during this stage (and prevent them from becoming catastrophic). The human failure typically occurs in either execution or opposition. The system failure is often related to governance, finances, and human resources. While this isn't an exhaustive list of potential oxygen tank fires, it will help prevent a lot of failure points.

Human Failure: Sabotage

Hopefully, through town halls and one-on-ones, you were able to address some of the change reactions before launching. But that's typically the first wave. The next wave comes when change starts. This is because it moves from being theoretical to something that is real. This can kick people's anxiety into high gear. But let's remember why it causes anxiety: fear. Fear of loss. Fear that the church of their childhood will no longer exist or that all their favorite things will be ripped away from them. Their reactions will be emotional rather than rational. Unfortunately, you can't really argue with emotion.

I have no objective data to back this up, but it feels that every decision in the life of the church is emotional on some level. Very successful, capable, rational people can lose it quickly. I think it's because faith, and memories of the people and events of the past, are inherently personal. This is why you'll get some red-faced responses and irate emails in your inbox as you lead change.

It's important to remember that this is a normal part of leading change. The important thing is how you respond when opposition gets loud. First, you want to do what Carey Nieuwhof suggests in his book *Leading Change without Losing It*: "do the math."[10] Just because change opponents make the most noise doesn't mean they represent a majority (or even a significant minority) of people in your congregation. Of course, they'll say things like, "Everyone is saying" or "A lot of people agree" or "I'm hearing from a lot of people." Usually, that just means them. Or maybe one or two of their friends.

Nieuwhof explains typical change reaction through the lens "of how four people-groups respond to something like the introduction of the latest smartphone."[11] There are early adopters, people who "enthusiastically embrace and adopt change."[12] These are the raving fans who are camping out in line to get the new phone, and they represent 10 percent of potential phone buyers. Then there's the early majority, people who are positive about change and will get the phone but don't need it the first day. This represents a larger 30 percent of buyers. Then, there's the quiet majority—"They're waiting to see where the culture goes and ultimately, they'll follow it."[13] This represents another 50 percent. Last are the opponents, representing the final 10 percent of potential buyers.

You'll discover that when you lead change, roughly 90 percent of people will buy the phone. Just because the other 10 percent is the loudest doesn't mean it's the largest. The point is, it almost always feels like it is. No matter what you do, there will be some who just aren't along for the ride. So what do you do with that 10 percent?

Opponents take many different forms: *stick in the mud, silent pot-stirrer, loud pot-stirrer, opposition party leader,* etc. They will use their resources and influence to stop the change from happening. Sometimes they're passive-aggressive, and other times they're just aggressive. Sabotage is the shrapnel of anger and grief. This is a reality that can cause critical rocket failure. But it shouldn't surprise you. Tod Bolsinger, in *Canoeing the Mountains*, has a helpful section on sabotage (I encourage you to read it), but the main thing is to expect it, embrace it as "a normal part of organizational life,"[14] and "don't take it personally."[15]

Occasionally, opponents will threaten to exit or try to organize an exit en masse. If that happens, try to get them to sit down and share their concerns. Sometimes, they just want to be heard. Then, if it's something you can address, agree to address it and give them a timetable of when you'll address it. This can prevent an exodus and, oddly, create unity because they felt you listened. They may still not like the change, but they usually agree to roll with it.

In the end, there will be some opponents who demand that you cease and desist. Sometimes, opponents just aren't willing to go forward with the change. It's not that they're dumb or obstinate; they just don't agree on the direction. When that happens, it may be the case that they need to move on and find a church home that better fits their felt needs (which is perfectly fine).

As you deal with change opponents, "never waver in your underlying principles."[16] Make sure you "prayerfully, biblically, and regularly evaluate your boundaries."[17] And do what you can to "move forward slowly and carefully,"[18] building as much consensus as possible. If people decide to leave, bless them. Like Paul and Barnabas, two godly people can sometimes reach a vision impasse. It almost always hurts when people leave, but it never hurts as much as the sabotage that can happen if they don't. Trust that God has different plans for them.

But sometimes, even when you prevent or correct the human failure points, you still find that your plan is malfunctioning. Like rocket launches, mechanical or system failure is the most common culprit. In church launches, it's often outdated or inadequate systems that prevent the rocket from leaving the atmosphere. Like a rubber band, it just snaps back to the ground. Below are a few common system failures when leading change.

System Failure: Scarcity Thinking

There is nothing that will slow you down more quickly than funding problems. Honestly, the worst of them is scarcity thinking. Resources almost always lag behind vision. That's a good thing. Why? Because it forces us to depend on God's provision (which is a good place to be). Do you believe God is driving your ministry goals? Then why don't you think God will fund them? Are you operating as if God will show up with the funding you need when you'll need it? I'm not talking about counting the cost. God gave us brains for a reason. But either we're trusting God or we're not. I'm amazed at how quickly counting the cost turns into an excuse not to trust.

Right out of seminary, I took a position as the solo pastor of a small Presbyterian church in central New Jersey. About two years in, the vision was to launch a contemporary worship service on Sunday morning, right after the traditional service. The problem was that we had no money. When I say no money, I truly mean zero. To make the service possible, we needed a sound system that could handle guitars, vocals, and so on. Our elders prayed together and concluded: *If God wants this, God will have to provide the money.*

Guess what? God did. We had a five-thousand-dollar bequest after a longtime member passed away. The elders told me, "Okay, here's five thousand dollars. Go get your sound system." If you know anything about audiovisual gear, you also know that five thousand dollars won't get you very far. But it was what God gave us to work with. So I made a list of essential gear and drove to Guitar Center in Edison, New Jersey, to start putting pieces together. I had no clue how we were going to pull this off, but I kept praying: *God, if you want this to work, I know you'll provide.*

As I looked at mixing boards, power amps, and speakers, a man walked into the store and started talking about gear with the clerk. It was obvious he'd been there a million times—*maybe a sales rep?* When he saw me looking, he came over and said: "I'm not sure why, but I feel like you need some help."

"Is it that obvious?" I laughed. I went on to explain the situation and how our church was trying to launch a new service. When I mentioned the purpose, his whole face changed, and he shook his head.

"You're a pastor?" he asked.

"Is it that obvious?" I repeated. We both laughed.

Then, he said, "Why did you have to be a pastor? Now I have to help you!" It turns out John Jackson was a man of God. And he built sound systems for a living. He asked what our budget was.

"Five thousand dollars," I said.

"I've got you," he responded, and he proceeded to multiply our five thousand dollars like audiovisual loaves and fishes.

You've got to resist scarcity thinking—if God wants it, God will give you what you need. It may not be a Cadillac, but a Corolla will do just fine. If you trust your way through funding fears, God will show up. But you also don't have to wait for someone to pass away to fund the vision.

System Failure: Giving

Whether you need to raise capital funds or bolster your operating budget, the strategy to increase giving has everything to do with sharing God's movement. It used to be in many churches that giving was pre-decided. Congregants would fill out pledge cards on stewardship Sunday—promising to pay a certain amount for that particular year. That's how most churches built their annual budgets. But nowadays, people give differently. Younger generations are more motivated by inspiration than obligation.

Think of those Sarah McLachlan commercials to save the animals. Donors aren't pitched on the cost of dog food, electric bills, or staff salaries at the shelter (the funding needs). They're shown images of mistreated animals while hearing Sarah sing "In the Arms of an Angel." They are moved by the need and inspired to do something about it.

Maybe you're thinking that this is a problem because it undermines the biblical teaching about tithing. It doesn't have to. What does Jesus say is most important about giving? The heart behind it (see the Sermon on the Mount). Inspiration is how you engage the heart and help people see how giving is part of their discipleship. You can (and should) teach about giving as a spiritual discipline, but that's just not the starting point for younger generations.

Their main driver of generosity, as J. Clif Christopher points out in *Not Your Parents' Offering Plate*, is that they "want to be a part of something that *changes lives*."[19] They want to make a difference. They want to see how their money drives the mission. How do you optimize your giving system to accomplish this?

The most powerful way is to share stories of life transformation and how people's giving helps make these stories possible.

Talk about the teenagers who built a wheelchair ramp on their mission trip—and the reaction of the resident as she went outside for the first time in four months. Share the faith story of the middle-aged man who decided to get baptized after years of running away from God, or the college student who came to church hungry to know Jesus. If you connect giving with the stories, generosity will increase. Again, find ways to bake it into what you're already doing.

We begin every staff meeting and elder meeting with what we call God sightings (a phrase we picked up from Group Workcamps decades ago). It's a simple way to invite people to share what God is doing. It's like a switch. Once people start looking for God sightings, they start seeing God's work everywhere. That's the lever you want to pull for your congregation. But before jumping to the next system, it's important to mention not just why people give, but how they give.

Study after study shows that even your most regular attenders come less often than they did even five or ten years ago. If giving is tethered to physical attendance, it will also be irregular. One of the biggest game-changing developments has been the advent of recurring online giving. When you set up recurring online giving, it's consistent, reliable, and never misses a Sunday. Half-jokingly, I regularly tell my congregation, "Recurring giving is great, because your money is here even when you're not."

Your church probably already has this set up. And it's most likely underutilized. The irony is that most younger generations prefer online giving anyway. They pay bills automatically through online checking accounts, and they use Venmo, QR codes, and PayPal for routine goods and services. So why are you relying on cash in a plate?

System Failure: Budgeting

If your giving system fails, you won't be able to fund the vision. But there's a next step that's just as important—how you allocate that funding: the budgeting process. In Chapter Six, we talked about the all-in church that only budgeted fifteen hundred dollars for youth ministry. At some point, you need to put your resources behind the changes God is calling you to make. A big obstacle is that most churches operate with entitlement budgets.

Show me the budget of a church, and I'll show you what it really values. Entitlement budgets are built on preserving the existing resource allocations. For example, let's say office supplies got five hundred dollars last year. The starting point for the budget for a new year will most likely be five hundred dollars. The church administrator, in an attempt to show the value of office supplies to the organization, will ask for a percentage increase every year. If it looks like only $350 will be spent, they'll feel pressured to spend the rest or else they might lose that money the following year.

This creates a siloed budget in which each ministry area is competing for resources. There's virtually no room for new projects or initiatives to get funded. When that happens, the rocket loses fuel and crashes to the ground. An entitlement budget begins with the question: *What did we spend last year?* A better approach is a vision budget that begins with: *What is God calling us to do this year?*

Let's say that your most important KRA is that reimagined Sunday school program. Start the budget process by asking: *How much money will it take to do what we need to do? Will we need a capital campaign? Will we need to add a staff position?* Then, whatever that number is, make that the first building block of your budget.

Then, start adding everything else back into the budget while asking, *How much will we need to save to fund the vision?* Ask each ministry area, *How can you contribute to the overall vision this year?* This promotes unity instead of resource competition. The funny thing is, the budget will end up looking largely the same as the entitlement budget. You'll still need to fund most of things you're already funding. But you start with a more faithful question, and this keeps the why at the center of everything.

System Failure: Decision-Making

When you accepted the call to your church, you inherited a governance system—a structure for decision-making and authority. This, by and large, is a good thing. However, it can become a failure point when decision-making gets too bogged down by complexity. Why? Because it slows down the ability to make changes at an effective speed. There's a litmus test for organizational efficiency that is an imperfect but useful diagnostic: you should be able to make a major decision within twenty-four hours. In most churches, it's more like twenty-four days.

The analogy I hear most often is that the church is like a cruise ship: it takes a long time to turn around. But just because the organization is a big ship doesn't mean it has to be so painfully slow to maneuver. Pastor Tim Clark discusses how the church should be more like a battleship. "A cruise ship, by definition, is designed for the comfort of the passengers. Even in a critical rescue situation, getting the vessel to turn 180 degrees will take at least ten to fifteen minutes and anything faster would create huge problems,"[20] both for the comfort of the people and the onboard systems. "A battleship, however, can turn much more quickly, in one to three minutes,"[21] which is sometimes the "difference between life and death."[22]

How do you speed up decision-making? First, you make it as local (and nimble) as possible. Could you imagine what would happen if a big ship had to wait for a decision by a committee before making every turn? It would hit a few icebergs. A better solution would be for the committee to set turning guidelines and let the crew steer as they need to within those parameters. If you have an elder board (or something similar), chances are they are micromanaging most boat turns. A better way is to let your staff and volunteers make the decisions locally, since they're the ones steering the boat.

System Failure: Volunteers

Volunteer support is more than just execution efficiency (mentioned earlier); it's the whole system of how you recruit, connect, and schedule them. Most churches feel they don't have enough volunteers to do the work, but what if that's more of a system problem than a people problem? For example, after the pandemic, some of our weekly and regular volunteers not only didn't return to volunteer, but they didn't return to church at all. Do you know what that tells me? They didn't miss it. Maybe they felt burned out. Maybe they didn't know how to get out of the commitment, like they were serving a life sentence. The remedy is to make sure we're lining up right-sized tasks with right-sized asks.

The way you do that is to make sure there's clarity around the what (we need you to serve in our nursery one Sunday morning a month; please arrive fifteen minutes before the first service, etc.). If you're not clear, the volunteer may feel stuck, or worse, like they weren't needed. Then, don't forget to thank and encourage them, to make them feel like the important part of the team that they truly are.

Yes, there are a lot of things that can go boom in your launch. But that's part of the normal process. If you have the discipline, you'll be able to successfully execute the plan. The next questions are: How will you know if the plan is working? How will you know if it's successful? Through measuring outcomes and pivoting, if necessary.

Chapter Twelve

FAITHFUL AND FRUITFUL

I am the vine; you are the branches. If you remain in me and I in you, you will bear much fruit; apart from me you can do nothing.

—JOHN 15:5

Why God chose humanity as Plan A to bring the gospel to the world is, in my view, one of the biggest mysteries of life. I'm not sure if you've noticed, but we're a bit of a mess. Every perfect, beautifully crafted KRA that you've spent weeks or months meticulously planning will depend on imperfect people to execute. Treasures in clay jars. Even though you've taken steps to mitigate human and systems failure, you won't always be able to eradicate it.

Just expect that things will get a little messy from time to time. It doesn't stop God from trusting us, so it shouldn't stop you either. But learning how to navigate it will help prevent mission failure. You'll have volunteers back out, flake out, or take a timeout. Or sometimes, they'll fail to do what they were trained or expected to do. Don't get too upset. Take a breath. Nine times out of ten, the execution can be fixed, and it's usually through pretty minimal adjustments.

If you watch sports at all, you know that the thing that makes or breaks a game, or even a player's career trajectory, isn't whether or not they make mistakes (they all do). It's how they recover from those mistakes. The person who has the greatest influence on that recovery is the coach. In football, for example, if a running back fumbles, a coach might take him out of the game the next play (often yelling at him on his way to the bench). This is a confidence killer. If it happens a couple of times, that player is never the same—they tend to be tight and anxious, and they often make more mistakes.

The best coaches, however, instead of yelling and benching them the first time, will wrap their arm around the player, give him a pep talk, and send him right back onto the field. Often, he'll get the ball again the very next play. Why? To show him: *Hey, you made a mistake, but I still believe in you—and we're going to need you to if we hope to win the game.*

Your team will have some fumbles. Don't be shocked by it. Don't bench the player (if you can help it). Like a good coach, remind them of the proper technique, give them a vote of confidence, and get them back in the game. Remember, you're going to need them if you hope to win. When a team member doesn't do something they were supposed to or misses a deadline, a good approach is something like: *I noticed that [fill in the blank] didn't get done; how can I help you do it?* Or, *I'm worried. I didn't set you up to succeed. What happened? How can I better support you?* You want to acknowledge that the outcomes are not meeting expectations. But you want to do it in a way that doesn't take them out of the game.

But how do you know when the ball has been fumbled? How do you know if your offense is moving the ball? You have to measure the results, and depending on what you find, you may need to adjust accordingly. This brings us to the final step of the Deploy stage: evaluating outcomes.

Sifting through the Drama

Aside from his advice to *be a tourist* when leading change, Jon Acuff also reminds us to "trust data, not drama."[1] And, yes, there'll be some drama (especially if it's a big change). Again, it's the shrapnel of fear and grief. When we changed our sanctuary in 2015, a lifelong member handed me a five-page document and said, "What you're doing is wrong." It was a typed, single-spaced printout of all the scriptures that warned against desecrating the temple or keeping the temple holy. *Thanks for the encouragement.*

When drama happens, you'll be tempted to compromise the plan to turn the temperature down on the emotional heat. This is because you care (and that's good). But a bigger mistake would be to stop moving forward because of it. My sixteen-year-old son's doctor has a saying (which I love): "Don't stack dumb on top of dumb." Every year at his annual physical, the doctor warns him about the pressures of drinking, drugs, and sex. His point is that everyone makes mistakes. At some point, years down the road, he might go to a party and have too much to drink, for example. That's dumb. But don't get behind the wheel after that. That's dumb on top of dumb. That's when terrible things happen.

Drama is normal, but don't let it stop you from faithful execution of the plan that you and your team prayerfully, thoughtfully, and diligently worked through together. That's dumb on top of dumb. I'm not saying don't respond or consider the criticism; just don't give it an inordinate amount of power. Remember who you're trying to reach and why you're not reaching them. Remember your mission. Remember what's at stake. Remember what can be lost in translation. Remember that just because a few people get dramatic doesn't mean you need to cancel the plans (remember, the loudest group isn't the largest). But you do need to have a good framework to measure the outcomes—it's the data that tells you how it's going. You can't manage what you don't measure. So let's talk about how you do it (and what to do if the outcomes aren't measuring up).

Measuring Outcomes: The Fruit Test

The two most important metrics to pay attention to, in this entire process, are faithfulness and fruitfulness. They go hand in hand; one begets the other. *Are we being faithful to the* Missio Dei *call to translate the wonders of God into the language of the people? Is that faithfulness producing fruit?* This isn't particularly earth-shattering, I know. But one of the biggest challenges that churches face is how to discern good fruit from bad.

In Matthew 7, Jesus teaches his disciples how to distinguish a false prophet from a legitimate one—or, how to practice spiritual discernment. He gives them a simple litmus test: *Just look at the fruit they produce.* Jesus explains, "Every good tree bears good fruit, but a bad tree bears bad fruit. . . . Thus, by their fruit you will recognize them" (Matt. 7:17, 20). I think a faithful principle can be extracted here: You can judge spiritual health by the quality of the fruit.

What does high-quality, God-sized fruit look like? It looks like Jesus. Bearing fruit is a result of discipleship. The more we conform to Christ, the more our fruit will resemble him. But how will we know if we're producing this fruit? It will look like the fruit of the Spirit: "love, joy, peace, forbearance, kindness, goodness, faithfulness, gentleness and self-control" (Gal. 5:22–23). If the fruit of our ministry production looks like this, we're bearing good fruit.

You may ask, *What does kindness or forbearance or peace have to do with ministry outcomes?* It's a nuanced approach, to be sure. But for me, it's asking: *How in this particular ministry are we generating one or more of these things in people's hearts and lives? How is Sunday school generating this fruit? How are women's circles or men's groups or potlucks generating this fruit?* Again, bearing fruit is what discipleship does. So if it's there, that's an important outcome to measure.

But according to Jesus in John 15, it's not just about the quality of the fruit but the quantity of fruit. He tells us that he is the "true vine" (v. 1), we are the "branches" (v. 5), and his Father is the "gardener" (v. 1). Jesus explains that the gardener's purpose is to grow the most fruit possible—planting and pruning for output.

Every summer, we vacation in Vermont. It's a small camp on Lake Champlain that is surrounded by apple orchards. The trees are all different shapes, as each one is meticulously pruned for maximum production. There are so many apples growing from them, it almost looks like piles of fruit stacked on each branch. In the Father's garden, the only way for branches to bear fruit like that (Jesus explains) is to "remain" (John 15:4) in the vine (and the Father will do the rest). This brings me to a second principle: you can judge spiritual health by the quality and quantity of the fruit.

The second question you'll ask of each ministry is: *Could it bear more fruit?* If the answer is yes, ask, *How can you adjust the ministry to bear more fruit, or is there something else that could bear more in its place?* It's precisely here that we are at risk of losing our way. Yes, healthy things grow: bodies, organizations, and churches. Growth is a logical next step for vine and branch flourishing. However, when churches measure outcomes, there is invariably an overemphasis on numerical growth. Numbers can quickly become either an idol or a false indicator of health. After all, unhealthy things grow, too.

For example, if sin is left unchecked, it can spread everywhere fast, like poison ivy in the garden. As Karl Vaters puts it in *De-Sizing the Church*: "When the numbers stay up, they capture our attention, blinding us to what might really be going on in the church, including in the pastor's own walk with God. If all healthy things grow, the [false] assumption is that all church growth is healthy."[2] Whether it's our American obsession with numbers or our desire to be on a "winning" team, the numbers metric can be a trap. Numbers may not reveal faithfulness or fruitfulness.

I don't think this comes from a bad place. After all, it's a pretty straightforward metric (one of the few), and it does tell a story. A big part of the story of Tower Hill church (that I've shared throughout this book) has been its numerical growth. But it's not growth for the sake of a crowd (at least I hope not); it's growth for the sake of a transformational relationship with Jesus. The *telos* of numerical growth is greater Christlikeness for a growing number of people. This propels God's mission forward.

Donald McGavran, one of the most prominent missiologists of the twentieth century (and godfather of the church growth movement), "taught that non-Christians should not be asked to hurdle major cultural barriers to become believers."[3] It's this foundation that led to the Willow Creek "seeker church" movement that inspired the attractional model of churches like North Point, Life.Church, and many others. It's the logical and, I'll argue, faithful attempt at taking James at the Council of Jerusalem (Acts 15) seriously.

But an inherent flaw in the attractional model is that it's intentionally built upon our consumerist impulses, which are often antithetical to the impulses of the Spirit. Kent Carlson and Mike Lueken, in their book, *Renovation of the Church*, state it strongly: "Attracting people to church based on their consumer demands is in direct and irredeemable conflict with inviting people, in Jesus' words, to lose their lives in order to find them."[4] This was born from their own experience in leading an attractional church. On the one hand, I completely agree. The church should not be reduced to a purveyor of religious goods and services trying to win a weekly popularity contest. We don't want it an inch deep and a mile wide.

And yet, I find a tension in it. Why? Because, although we do want it deeper, we still want it wide. Personally, I don't want to lead a church as far as the attractional model wants, or even demands, to go. But let me offer this defense. In a way, this is exactly what we've been talking about with leveraging culture to translate the gospel. Isn't the goal to reach young families (or any other demographic) so they can hear the wonders of God in their own language? How do you reach them if they're not in the room? We should have a burning desire to proclaim the good news to as many as possible.

The problem, in my view, is when the model exists to feed itself. It's when the quality of the fruit is sacrificed for the quantity. Numbers become the only metric that matters, the metric upon which the entire ministry is evaluated. Success is always up and to the right. More equals winning. That can lead to some pretty gross outcomes.

For example, I was talking to a friend who shared a story about a middle-aged woman who attended a megachurch in North Carolina. This church, by the way, is a spectacle to behold. They, like many churches that size, have cracked the code on connecting with people. They are incredible at it. I always am trying to learn how they do it so we can get better at it in our context.

Here's where it goes south. The woman was able to find a seat in the first or second row; she was excited to be so close to the stage. But a few minutes before service, a staff member approached her and told her that she had to move because she was in the camera shots for the live broadcast. When she asked why that was a problem, the staff member apologized and explained that they only wanted young people sitting up front. Now, I'm sure they had a well-thought-out strategy that made perfect sense to them. However, it seems like someone let some bad fruit flourish.

Listen, it's not that numbers are bad—I don't know any pastor that would rather preach to an empty room. There's a line I heard once that I really like: numbers count because people matter. These are lives we're talking about. These are, potentially, people making decisions to follow Jesus. But if numbers are the constant focus, it's not going to work. I'll come back to Karl Vaters here, as he rightly nails the problem on the head: "From the pride it brings when the numbers are up to the shame and frustration it causes when the numbers are static or down, none of this provides a healthy foundation on which to build a healthy church body."[5]

There's a balance we need to fight for. We need to make disciples. We need to go deep and wide. We're not just picking on megachurches. We're also exposing small churches that refuse to even try to reach beyond their walls, churches that care more about preserving their customs than sharing Jesus with the next generation. We need the best of both, and we need to discard the rest. As Andy Stanley puts it, "Healthy local churches can be, and should be, both deep and wide. It's not either/or. It's both/and. . . . Churches should be theologically sound and culturally relevant."[6]

Between the McGavran church growth movement side and the necessary discipleship corrective of the last ten to twenty years, I'll borrow a line from Oliver Stone's *Platoon*: "There are times since, I have felt like the child born of those two fathers."[7] What's the right way to measure the outcomes? With balance. It's about faithfulness and fruitfulness. That fruitfulness is both in quality and quantity.

The Four Types of Growth

In Acts 2, numerical growth is an outcome of church health. But it's not the only one. We started this process with the thunder and fire of Pentecost, so perhaps it's only fitting that we return to Acts 2 to see what a flourishing community of faith looks like. This Spirit-born *ekklesia* can provide a helpful framework to measure faithfulness and fruitfulness. Bob Whitesel and Kent Hunter, in *A House Divided*, break down Acts 2:43–47 into four types of growth for churches to evaluate. The first is based on verses 42–43: maturity.

> They devoted themselves to the apostles' teaching and to fellowship, to the breaking of bread and to prayer. (Acts 2:42–43)

"The significance of its members' devotion to teaching and fellowship, combined with the attesting miracles, testifies to a congregation maturing in its understanding and practice of spiritual principles."[8] But how do you measure maturity? In the end, it's always a bit subjective. One way is to measure engagement. Most churches have church management software that they're underutilizing. Did you know you could use it to track engagement? You're probably already using it to track giving. Start migrating your Bible study, worship, and Sunday school attendance to the software. Then you can get an idea of how engaged someone is. Once a year, go back and reevaluate and ask: *Did that person become more engaged, less engaged, or stay the same?* Engagement doesn't always lead to maturity, but it's a start.

What you're really trying to capture is discipleship growth. Set up the indicators that help you see discipleship outcomes: giving, small groups, Bible study, and mission and volunteer activity. The next type of church growth is based on verses 44–47: unity.

> All the believers were together and had everything in common. They sold property and possessions to give to anyone who had need. Every day they continued to meet

> together in the temple courts. They broke bread in their homes and ate together with glad and sincere hearts, praising God. (Acts 2:44–47)

Unity, like maturity, is a subjective thing to measure. In many ways, it's a feel for the pulse of the congregation. "The early church drew together in a unity and harmony that led to selfless acts of inter-reliance."[9] But how do you measure oneness? I think it starts by assessing the degree to which different church constituencies or generations or factions operate with an "us vs. them" mentality. Is there a consensus in the mission, vision, and strategy of the church? Or is there some division, or even hostility? When asked to contribute, either physically or financially, is it a constant uphill battle? Or are people excited to engage?

The next type of growth, favor, is based on verse 47: ". . . and enjoying the favor of all the people." This measurement "indicates the extent to which a church is establishing and maintaining a positive image and mutual respect in the community."[10] It's about the reputation of your church and relationships within it. Here's an important question: If your church were no longer there, would the community (people who aren't part of the church) miss it? In other words, do people value what you do and see you as an important community presence? That's favor.

I happen to think that the perfect Christian song is "Jesus, Friend of Sinners" by Casting Crowns. I think we should all play it on repeat every single day (really). There are lyrics in the song I always think of when I think of favor:

> Nobody knows what we're for
> Only what we're against when we judge the wounded.
> What if we put down our signs, crossed over the lines
> and love like you did?[11]

Does your community know what you're for? Do they know that you are for them? Measuring favor is evaluating the quality and quantity of your community relationships. Every year, we send volunteers to help a local firemen's fair that raises money for the volunteer fire department. We run the carnival games for a few hours on a couple of nights just to be helpful neighbors—plus, it's really fun. This has generated such a harvest of goodwill toward the church because the fire department and community see that we're here for them (even if they never come to church).

Last, the fourth growth outcome is numbers: "And the Lord added to their number daily those who were being saved" (Acts 2:47). I don't know whether or not there's a deeper reason, but I like that it's the fourth on the list. But you can't ignore it. Clearly, numbers are a key part of painting the picture of faithfulness and fruitfulness.

What Happens If the Picture Isn't Good?

I hate to even say it, because I know how hard it is to hear. After all this work, all this time, and all this energy, what if the outcomes aren't what you're hoping or expecting? What if you feel like your KRA missed the mark? Or what if it stalled out mid-flight? First, let me encourage you. If you did the work, you're already in a better position than you would have been. Adjusting strategies is a lot faster (and easier) than determining vision. Second, it will most likely lead to something even more effective than what you had in mind. So don't lose heart.

In basketball, the pivot foot is the key to success. From the pivot, you can get into a more favorable position to dribble, pass, or shoot—all three possibilities. Just because you have the ball doesn't mean you have the right angle to move forward. But if you pivot, you can find your way. Let me give you an example.

In 2018, we decided that we wanted to try and reach young families who had significant youth sports commitments that kept them out of Sunday morning engagement. So we had the idea to start a worship experience at five o'clock in the evening. We called it Tower Hill Nights. It was a stripped-down, acoustic service that was intentionally shorter than the Sunday morning service. Instead of holding it in our sanctuary, we held it in our renovated youth space because we wanted a more casual, kid-friendly environment—and it gave it a cool, coffeehouse vibe.

The room fits about eighty-five to ninety people packed together. We regularly got fifty to sixty, so it felt full. It quickly became the staff's favorite service. I think this is because they didn't have to worry about Sunday school or other Sunday morning duties. Everyone loved the format. Well, almost everyone. Guess who never really came? Young families with youth who played sports.

We discovered that, despite their verbal intentions to come, by the time they finished sports on Sunday, they were wiped. They didn't go back out to do much of anything. If a family had older kids, it was prime homework time. If they had younger kids, there were risks of meltdowns. Who were the fifty to sixty people? They were double-dippers. People who came on Sunday morning and then came back again. It was the same (albeit shorter) sermon too, which was a little odd.

After a few months in, we realized that it was a lot of work to pull off a Sunday evening service when we were already worn out from Sunday morning. We had to admit, it wasn't delivering what we hoped. So we pulled the plug. We didn't pull it because it was unsuccessful. We pulled it because it missed the target, and if we had kept going, it would have taken away resources from the thing that would hit the target. Eventually, we moved to adding another service on Sunday morning to provide a later morning time. This hit our goal better. But we never could have done it if we were burning fuel for Tower Hill Nights.

If your KRA isn't hitting the goal, maybe it needs adjusting. Or maybe it needs to end so the right thing can start. I think this has to do with holding your plans loosely. Let them breathe. Evaluate them honestly, and pivot if you have to. Again, sometimes you're a pivot or two away from breakthrough. Treat your church like a ministry lab. Experiments don't always yield expected results. But you'll never know unless you test them.

Doing Hard Things Doesn't Have to Be Hard on You

Hopefully, from this process, you've gleaned the absolute necessity of sharing the work. Don't go it alone. As the primary vision carrier, you'll be tempted to carry too much. Don't do it. You'll become the lid on the growth of your church. It's because the church will only grow according to your capability. That's not biblical, nor is it healthy for anyone, especially you.

My advice is to take care of yourself along the way. Take vacations. Make strong boundaries (and keep them) to protect you and your family. Try not to take yourself too seriously. Laugh a lot. Have fun. Keep a winsome spirit about leading change. And be yourself. God chose you—not Andy Stanley, Tim Keller, or anyone else—to lead your church. He wants you to be you. Trust that it's your voice God wants to use.

Yes, the work of revitalization is hard. You, and your church, will need some resilience and intestinal fortitude. You'll need some backbone. You'll need heart. You'll need to trust in God's plan even when you can't see the road ahead. Trust in the thunder and fire of God's presence to transform trembling Jesus followers into Jesus proclaimers. Trust as God hands his Word to the next generation through you, empowering you to do what only God can do.

The mission is worth the risk and discomfort. So translate well, my brothers and sisters. Help the next generation grow in maturity, unity, favor, and numbers. Help them bear fruit for the generations after them. Let's make sure the greatest news the world has ever known doesn't get lost in translation. Let's make sure we speak their language.

Notes

Chapter 1

1. Idea taken from: Adam Hamilton, *24 Hours That Changed the World* (Abingdon Press, 2009).
2. Timothy Keller, *Center Church: Doing Balanced, Gospel-Centered Ministry in Your City* (Zondervan, 2012), 93.
3. Daniel L. Migliore, *Faith Seeking Understanding: An Introduction to Christian Theology* (Eerdmans, 2004), 198.
4. "Spirituality among Americans," Pew Research Center, December 7, 2023, https://www.pewresearch.org/religion/2023/12/07/spirituality-among-americans/.
5. Jake Meador, "The Misunderstood Reason Millions of Americans Stopped Going to Church," *The Atlantic*, July 29, 2023, https://www.theatlantic.com/ideas/archive/2023/07/christian-church-communitiy-participation-drop/674843/.
6. "Presbyterian Church (USA)," n.d., https://pcusa.org/resources/statistics-lists.
7. Aaron Earls, "New Normal Settles for Churches Post-Pandemic," *Lifeway Research*, November 14, 2023, https://research.lifeway.com/2023/11/14/new-normal-settles-for-churches-post-pandemic/.
8. David Beckworth and Paul J. Olson, "Religious Change and Stability: Seasonality in Church Attendance from the 1940s to the 2000s," *Journal for the Scientific Study of Religion* 50, no. 2 (2011): 388–96.
9. Darrell L. Guder, ed., *Missional Church: A Vision for the Sending of the Church in North America* (Eerdmans, 1998), 48.
10. Leah MarieAnn Klett, "43% of Millennials 'Don't Know, Don't Care, Don't Believe' God Exists: Study," *The Christian Post*, May 19, 2021, https://www.christianpost.com/news/millennials-dont-know-dont-care-dont-believe-god-exists.html/.

11. John Kotter, *Leading Change* (Harvard Business Review Press, 2012), 28.
12. Steps adapted from Kotter, *Leading Change.*

Chapter 2

1. Max De Pree, *Leadership Is an Art* (Doubleday, 1989), 9.
2. John Kotter, *Leading Change* (Harvard Business Review Press, 2012), 28.
3. Jim Collins, *Good to Great: Why Some Companies Make the Leap . . . and Others Don't* (Harper Business, 2001), 41.
4. Kotter, *Leading Change*, 37.
5. Kotter, *Leading Change*, 38.
6. Aaron Earls, "Online Services Expanded Reach of Churches During Pandemic," *Lifeway Research*, October 14, 2021, https://research.lifeway.com/2021/10/14/online-services-expanded-reach-of-churches-during-pandemic/.
7. Angela Haupt, "Is It Healthy to Weigh Yourself Every Day? A Look at the Pros and Cons," *The Washington Post*, February 2, 2022, https://www.washingtonpost.com/wellness/2022/02/01/pros-cons-weighing-yourself-daily/.
8. Haupt, "Is It Healthy to Weigh Yourself Every Day?"
9. Les McKeown, *Predictable Success: Getting Your Organization on the Growth Track—And Keeping It There* (Greenleaf Book Group Press, 2010), 16.
10. Tony Morgan, *The Unstuck Church: Equipping Churches to Experience Sustained Health* (Thomas Nelson, 2017), Kindle, 6.
11. Image used with permission from *Predictable Success: Getting Your Organization on the Growth Track—and Keeping It There*, copyright Les McKeown 2010–2025.

Chapter 3

1. Maya Mehrara, "What Is Gen Beta? How Babies Born from 2025 Will Change the World," *Newsweek*, January 1, 2025, https://www.newsweek.com/what-gen-beta-how-babies-born-2025-will-change-world-2008332/.
2. Mehrara, "What Is Gen Beta?"

3. Jean M. Twenge, *Generation Me: Why Today's Young Americans Are More Confident, Assertive, Entitled—and More Miserable Than Ever Before* (Free Press, 2006), 2.
4. Bob Whitesel and Kent R. Hunter, *A House Divided: Bridging the Generation Gaps in Your Church* (Abingdon Press, 2000), 20.
5. Whitesel and Hunter, *House Divided*, 41.
6. John Piper, "'Don't Waste Your Life': Seven Minutes That Moved a Generation," Desiring God, May 19, 2017, https://www.desiringgod.org/messages/boasting-only-in-the-cross/excerpts/dont-waste-your-life.
7. Bob Whitesel, *Preparing for Change Reaction: How to Introduce Change in Your Church* (Wesleyan, 2007), 54.
8. David Beckworth and Paul J. Olson, "Religious Change and Stability," *Journal for the Scientific Study of Religion* 50, no. 2 (June 2011): 388–96.
9. Whitesel and Hunter, *House Divided*, 56.
10. Erin Blakemore, "The Latchkey Generation: How Bad Was It?" *JSTOR Daily*, November 9, 2015, https://daily.jstor.org/latchkey-generation-bad/.
11. Shelbey Jumper, "The Lowdown on Cable Television," Clemson University, n.d., https://opentextbooks.clemson.edu/sts1010fidlerfall2022/chapter/the-lowdown-on-cable-television/.
12. Whitesel and Hunter, *House Divided*, 59.
13. Whitesel and Hunter, *House Divided*, 172.
14. Tim Elmore, *Generation iY: Secrets to Connecting with Today's Teens & Young Adults in the Digital Age* (Poet Gardener, 2015), Kindle, 39.
15. "Three Spiritual Journeys of Millennials," Barna, June 3, 2013, https://www.barna.com/research/three-spiritual-journeys-of-millennials/.
16. "Three Spiritual Journeys of Millennials."
17. Darrell E. Hall, *Speaking across Generations: Messages That Satisfy Boomers, Xers, Millennials, Gen Z, and Beyond* (IVP, 2022), Kindle, 34.
18. John Kotter, *Leading Change* (Harvard Business Review Press, 2012), 53.

Chapter 4

1. Amy Gallo, "What Is Active Listening?," *Harvard Business Review*, January 2, 2024, https://hbr.org/2024/01/what-is-active-listening/.
2. "Translation and Contextualization," Wycliffe Global Alliance, https://www.wycliffe.net/the-wycliffe-global-alliance-and-bible-translation-movements/translation-and-contextualization/.
3. Edward L. Greenstein, "Theories of Modern Bible Translation," *Prooftexts* 3, no. 1 (January 1983): 12. http://www.jstor.org/stable/20689053.
4. Christine M. Beckman and Melissa Mazmanian, *Dreams of the Overworked: Living, Working, and Parenting in the Digital Age* (Stanford University Press, 2020).
5. Beckman and Mazmanian, *Dreams of the Overworked*, 9.
6. Beckman and Mazmanian, *Dreams of the Overworked*, 47.
7. Beckman and Mazmanian, *Dreams of the Overworked*, 75.
8. Beckman and Mazmanian, *Dreams of the Overworked*, 11.
9. David Noel Freedman, "Areopagus," in *Anchor Bible Dictionary*, ed. David L. Tiede (Doubleday, 1992), 6:370.
10. John Kotter, *Leading Change* (Harvard Business Review Press, 2012), 69.
11. Timothy Keller, *Center Church: Doing Balanced, Gospel-Centered Ministry in Your City* (Zondervan, 2012), 18.
12. Keller, *Center Church*, 17.
13. Keller, *Center Church*, 17.
14. Gabriela Miranda, "Pandemic Babies' Parents Have Fears," *Asbury Park Press*, May 21, 2021.
15. Robert Schuller, *Peace of Mind through Possibility Thinking* (Doubleday, 1977), 102.

Chapter 5

1. Richard J. Foster, *Celebration of Discipline: The Path to Spiritual Growth* (HarperCollins, 1998), 158.
2. Dan Kimball, *The Emerging Church: Vintage Christianity for New Generations* (Zondervan, 2003), xiv.
3. Kimball, *Emerging Church*, xiv.

4. Bob Whitesel and Kent R. Hunter, *A House Divided: Bridging the Generation Gaps in Your Church* (Abingdon Press, 2000), 161.
5. Jannik Linder, "Visual Learner Statistics," Gitnux, April 29, 2025, https://gitnux.org/visual-learner-statistics/.
6. Andy Stanley, *Deep and Wide: Creating Churches Unchurched People Love to Attend* (Zondervan, 2012), 91.

Chapter 6

1. Leonardo Blair, "Christianity Is 'a Generation Away from Extinction' in Britain, Says Former Archbishop of Canterbury," *The Christian Post*, November 20, 2013, https://www.christianpost.com/news/christianity-is-a-generation-away-from-extinction-in-britain-says-former-archbishop-of-canterbury.html/.
2. "The Outpouring," Asbury University, https://www.asbury.edu/about/revival-history/outpouring/.
3. Jenn Johnson and Bethel Music, "Goodness of God," by Jenn Johnson, Ed Cash, Jason Ingram, Ben Fielding, and Brian Johnson, recorded in 2018, track 3 on *Victory*, Bethel Music, 2019.
4. "The Outpouring," Asbury University.
5. Kevin Brown, "What the Asbury Revival Taught Me about Gen Z," *Christianity Today*, March 2024, www.christianitytoday.com/2024/02/asbury-revival-taught-me-about-gen-z-casual-christianity/.
6. "The Outpouring," Asbury University.
7. Kevin Brown, "Uncertainty, Mission, and Holy Imagination," in *Cooperating with the Holy Spirit: A Theological and Practical Reflection on the Asbury Outpouring*, ed. Suzanne Nicholson (Abilene Christian University Press, 2025), Kindle, 187.
8. Brown, "What the Asbury Revival Taught Me about Gen Z."
9. "How Teens around the World Relate to Jesus," Barna, 2022, https://www.barna.com/the-open-generation/open-to-jesus/.
10. "How Teens around the World Relate to Jesus."
11. Brown, "What the Asbury Revival Taught Me about Gen Z."
12. "How Teens around the World Relate to Jesus."
13. "How Teens around the World Relate to Jesus."

14. "Openness to Jesus Isn't the Problem—the Church Is," Barna, May 17, 2023, https://www.barna.com/research/openness-to-jesus/.
15. "How Teens around the World Relate to Jesus."
16. "How Teens around the World Relate to Jesus."
17. "How Teens around the World Relate to Jesus."
18. "How Teens around the World Relate to Jesus."
19. "How Teens around the World Relate to Jesus."
20. J. Warner Wallace, *Truth in True Crime: What Investigating Death Teaches Us about the Meaning of Life* (Zondervan, 2024), 21.
21. Carl Trueman, "Obsession with Self-Identity, Sexuality, and Rewriting History," Broadcast Talks, C. S. Lewis Institute, August 15, 2022, https://www.cslewisinstitute.org/resources/obsession-with-self-identity-sexuality-and-rewriting-history-where-we-are/.
22. Trueman, "Obsession with Self-Identity."
23. "How Teens around the World Can Make an Impact," Barna, 2022, https://www.barna.com/the-open-generation/open-to-impact/.
24. Jeff Fromm and Angie Read, *Marketing to Gen Z: The Rules for Reaching This Vast and Very Different Generation of Influencers* (AMACOM, 2018), xx.
25. Kara Powell, Jake Mulder, and Brad Griffin, *Growing Young: 6 Essential Strategies to Help Young People Discover and Love Your Church* (Baker, 2016), 97.
26. Nancy Beach and Samantha Beach Kiley, *Next Sunday: An Honest Dialogue about the Future of the Church* (IVP, 2022), Kindle, 17.
27. Powell, Mulder, and Griffin, *Growing Young*, 168.
28. Fromm and Read, *Marketing to Gen Z*, 9.
29. Fromm and Read, *Marketing to Gen Z*, 23.
30. Powell, Mulder, and Griffin, *Growing Young*, 105.
31. Fromm and Read, *Marketing to Gen Z*, 56.
32. Powell, Mulder, and Griffin, *Growing Young*, 95.
33. Fromm and Read, *Marketing to Gen Z*, 69.

Chapter 7

1. "Jurassic World VelociCoaster at Universal's Islands of Adventure," Orlando Informer, last updated June 2, 2025, https://orlandoinformer.com/universal/jurassic-world-velocicoaster/.
2. *The Princess Bride*, directed by Rob Reiner (20th Century Fox, 1987).
3. Richard J. Mouw, *Abraham Kuyper: A Short and Personal Introduction* (Eerdmans, 2011), 4.
4. John Stott, *Christian Basics: An Invitation to Discipleship* (Baker, 2003), 14.
5. Stott, *Christian Basics*, 17.
6. "John Wesley's Conversion on Aldersgate Street," God's Missionary Church, https://godsmissionarychurch.org/2020/05/24/john-wesleys-salvation-testimony/.
7. Robert Wuthnow, *After Heaven: Spirituality in America since the 1950s* (University of California Press, 1998), 1.
8. Dallas Willard, *Renovation of the Heart: Putting on the Character of Christ* (NavPress, 2002), 19.
9. Willard, *Renovation of the Heart*, 22.
10. Marjorie J. Thompson, *Soul Feast: An Invitation to the Christian Spiritual Life* (Westminster John Knox Press, 2005), 7.
11. John Mark Comer, *Practicing the Way: Be with Jesus. Become Like Him. Do as He Did* (WaterBrook, 2024), 9.
12. "Frequently asked questions," Geocaching, https://www.geocaching.com/sites/education/en/frequently-asked-questions.
13. Andy Stanley and Bill Willits, *Creating Community: Five Keys to Building a Small Group Culture* (Multnomah, 2004), 116.
14. Stanley and Willits, *Creating Community*, 116.
15. Stanley and Willits, *Creating Community*, 117.
16. Stanley and Willits, *Creating Community*, 117.
17. Stanley and Willits, *Creating Community*, 118, emphasis mine.
18. Stanley and Willits, *Creating Community*, 118.
19. Stanley and Willits, *Creating Community*, 119, emphasis mine.

Chapter 8

1. Priscilla Pope-Levison, *Models of Evangelism* (Baker Academic, 2020), 5.
2. Pope-Levison, *Models of Evangelism*, 125.
3. Timothy Keller, *Center Church: Doing Balanced, Gospel-Centered Ministry in Your City* (Zondervan, 2012), 277.
4. "Damar Hamlin Timeline from Injury to Return to Bills," *Associated Press*, October 1, 2023, https://apnews.com/article/damar-hamlin-cardiac-arrest-nfl-comeback-f4fb672dd245f301d6c42891623f7e08/.
5. "'Pray for Damar': Wave of Public Prayer Follows Hamlin's Collapse," *PBS News*, January 7, 2023, https://www.pbs.org/newshour/nation/pray-for-damar-wave-of-public-prayer-follows-hamlins-collapse/.
6. Christian Pinkston, "From Super Bowl Ads to Kentucky Revivals, Stop the Christian Cannibalism," *Religion News Service*, February 27, 2023, https://religionnews.com/2023/02/27/from-super-bowl-ads-to-kentucky-revivals-stop-the-christian-cannibalism/.
7. Juan Martin Villegas, "He Gets Us," LERMA/, June 13, 2024, https://lermaagency.com/the-work/he-gets-us/.
8. Pinkston, "From Super Bowl Ads to Kentucky Revivals."
9. "Jesus Revolution," Box Office Mojo, https://www.boxofficemojo.com/release/rl466125569/.
10. Walker Hayes and Craig Allen Cooper, *Glad You're Here: Two Unlikely Friends Breaking Bread and Fences* (Moody, 2022), 23.
11. Walker Hayes, "Craig," track 10 on *Boom*, Monument, 2017.
12. Aaron Earls, "Most Open to Spiritual Conversations, Few Christians Speaking," *Lifeway Research*, February 22, 2022, https://research.lifeway.com/2022/02/22/most-open-to-spiritual-conversations-few-christians-speaking/.
13. Earls, "Most Open to Spiritual Conversations."
14. Penn Jillette, "A Gift of a Bible," *Penn Says*, episode 192, December 9, 2008.
15. Thom Rainer, *The Unchurched Next Door* (Zondervan, 2003), 24.

Chapter 10

1. "Starship," SpaceX, https://www.spacex.com/vehicles/starship/.
2. "Starship."
3. Clive Simpson, "How SpaceX's Starship Stacks Up to Other Rockets," *Spaceflight Now*, April 17, 2023, https://spaceflightnow.com/2023/04/17/how-spacexs-starship-stacks-up-to-other-rockets/.
4. "Status Quo Bias in Psychology: Why We Resist Change and How to Overcome It," *NeuroLaunch*, September 14, 2024, https://neurolaunch.com/status-quo-bias-psychology/.
5. Howard Schultz, *Onward: How Starbucks Fought for Its Life without Losing Its Soul* (Rodale Books, 2011), Kindle, 49.
6. Schultz, *Onward*, Kindle, 5.
7. Reggie McNeal, *A Work of Heart: Understanding How God Shapes Spiritual Leaders* (Jossey-Bass, 2011), xxi.
8. For the whole story on what we did, including a time-lapse of the transition, visit https://reclaimedleader.com/worship.
9. Lon Roberts, "Analysis Paralysis: A Case of Terminological Inexactitude," *Defense AT&L*, January–February 2010, https://web.archive.org/web/20161122195255/http://www.dau.mil/pubscats/ATL%20Docs/Jan-Feb/robersts_jan-feb10.pdf/.

Chapter 11

1. Robert Frost, "The Road Not Taken," *Atlantic Monthly*, August 1915.
2. Steven Pressfield, *The War of Art: Break Through the Blocks and Win Your Inner Creative Battles* (Black Irish Entertainment, 2012), 64.
3. Chris McChesney, Sean Covey, and Jim Huling, *The 4 Disciplines of Execution: Achieving Your Wildly Important Goals* (Simon & Schuster, 2021), 36.
4. McChesney, Covey, and Huling, *4 Disciplines of Execution*, 55.
5. McChesney, Covey, and Huling, *4 Disciplines of Execution*, 75.
6. McChesney, Covey, and Huling, *4 Disciplines of Execution*, 89.
7. "Apollo 13," *Britannica*, https://www.britannica.com/topic/Apollo-13-mission.

8. "Apollo 13."
9. "Apollo 13."
10. Carey Nieuwhof, *Leading Change without Losing It: Five Strategies That Can Revolutionize How You Lead Change When Facing Opposition* (The reThink Group, 2012), 33.
11. Nieuwhof, *Leading Change without Losing It*, 34.
12. Nieuwhof, *Leading Change without Losing It*, 34.
13. Nieuwhof, *Leading Change without Losing It*, 35.
14. Tod Bolsinger, *Canoeing the Mountains: Christian Leadership in Uncharted Territory* (IVP, 2015), 175–76.
15. Bolsinger, *Canoeing the Mountains*, 175–76.
16. Bob Whitesel, *Preparing for Change Reaction: How to Introduce Change in Your Church* (Wesleyan, 2007), 126.
17. Whitesel, *Preparing for Change Reaction*, 128.
18. Whitesel, *Preparing for Change Reaction*, 151.
19. J. Clif Christopher, *Not Your Parents' Offering Plate: A New Vision for Financial Stewardship* (Abingdon Press, 2008), 13.
20. "Turning a Big Ship Around," *Fueled by Pastor Tim Clark* (blog), https://www.pastortimclark.com/?p=4516/.
21. "Turning a Big Ship Around."
22. "Turning a Big Ship Around."

Chapter 12

1. I heard Jon Acuff say this at the Catalyst Conference in Atlanta, 2015.
2. Timothy Keller, *Center Church: Doing Balanced, Gospel-Centered Ministry in Your City* (Zondervan, 2012), 101.
3. Keller, *Center Church*, 187.
4. Kent Carlson and Mike Lueken, *Renovation of the Church: What Happens When a Seeker Church Discovers Spiritual Formation* (IVP, 2011), 35.
5. Karl Vaters, *De-Sizing the Church: How Church Growth Became a Science, Then an Obsession, and What's Next* (Moody, 2024), 12.
6. Andy Stanley, *Deep and Wide: Creating Churches Unchurched People Love to Attend* (Zondervan, 2012), 18.

7. Oliver Stone, dir., *Platoon* (Orion Pictures, 1986).
8. Bob Whitesel and Kent R. Hunter, *A House Divided: Bridging the Generation Gaps in Your Church* (Abingdon Press, 2000), 204.
9. Whitesel and Hunter, *House Divided*, 205.
10. Whitesel and Hunter, *House Divided*, 212.
11. Casting Crowns, "Jesus, Friend of Sinners," by Mark Hall and Matthew West, track 3 on *Come to the Well*, Beach Street / Reunion, 2011.